FORGOTTEN MANDATE

FORGOTTEN MANDATE

A BRITISH DISTRICT OFFICER
IN TANGANYIKA

E. K. LUMLEY

ARCHON BOOKS

1976

First published 1976 in the United Kingdom
by C. Hurst & Co. (Publishers) Ltd., London
and in the United States of America as an
Archon Book, an imprint of the Shoe String Press, Inc.,
Hamden, Connecticut 06514

© 1976 by E. K. Lumley

ISBN 0-208-01556-6

*Typeset in India by Tata Press, Ltd., Bombay,
and printed in Great Britain by Billing and Sons, Ltd.,
Guildford and London.*

CONTENTS

Author's Note   vii

1. Introduction   9

2. Indirect Rule in Tanganyika   14

3. Kibondo   21

4. Bugufi   32

5. The Source of the Nile   51

6. Lindi and Tunduru   54

7. Korogwe   60

8. Mbulu—the First Phase   75

9. Mbulu—the Second Phase   84

10. Lindi again   96

11. Kiberege   113

12. Bukoba   142

13. Finale   167

Autobiographical Epilogue   174

Index   179

AUTHOR'S NOTE

The material on which this book is based consists of my own contemporary records kept in diary form. When I had reshaped the material into a narrative, Sir Colin Coote was kind enough to read it, and my thanks are due to him for encouraging me in the belief that the content would be of general interest today, provided that some further reshaping were done. I must also express my thanks to Douglas Brown for his work in editing my manuscript and preparing it for publication. Without the advice and expertise of these two men, the book could never have been published.

1

INTRODUCTION

Colonialism, as the term is used today, means the political and administrative control exercised, for a brief period in history, by certain European nations over parts of the undeveloped world. It is unfashionable to give this episode much credit; be that as it may, since its winding-up in the aftermath of the Second World War, many people have forgotten how it actually functioned. The founding of the British and other colonial empires, their heyday and their eventual dissolution have often been described in terms of high politics. In terms of administration in the field, and of the contact there between two levels of progress, less has been written, although it is by this yardstick that the colonial interlude can best be judged.

Between 1923 and 1944 I was at this point of contact, doing the work of a District Commissioner. The place was Tanganyika which now, with Zanzibar, forms the Federal Republic of Tanzania, but which then was an ex-enemy territory mandated to Britain by the League of Nations. My brief derived from the Mandate, but it was in accord with Britain's colonial policy generally. Principally it was to further, before all else, the interests of the indigenous peoples of the region. A District Commissioner, or District Officer as he was sometimes called, occupied a comparatively lowly position in the colonial hierarchy. Nevertheless he was the effective agent of its policy, the man on whom the success or failure of that policy mainly depended.

For purposes of administration Tanganyika, like most other British colonial territories, was divided into Provinces and sub-divided into Districts. At the head of the Province was the Provincial Commissioner. Under him were the District Commissioners in charge of the Districts. Instructions on policy travelled from the Governor of the Territory through his Secretariat at Headquarters to the Provincial Commissioner and from him to every D.C. under his command.

The D.C. was the final link in the chain. He was at the grass-roots of administration, in direct contact with the tribal chiefs and their subjects. It was his responsibility to carry out government policy; no one was better placed to evaluate or diagnose the effect of that policy on the indigenous population. If it were unpopular he had to bear the brunt of tribal disapproval. If he knew it to be inappropriate, he could turn a deaf ear or blind eye to instructions from on high, but this was dangerous and could have unhappy personal repercussions. Generally, however, the D.C.'s advice was taken as to what should or should not be done in his District: he was, after all, the one who should know.

The District Commissioner had to be a man of many parts. To qualify for appointment to the administrative branch of the Colonial Service he had, in my time, to hold an honours degree in Arts from a recognised university. The majority of my contemporaries came from Oxford or Cambridge; a few, like myself, from Trinity College, Dublin. It helped the applicant's cause if, in addition to a good degree, he had some kind of athletic record. Bookworms were not considered good material for a job that called for great physical endurance. The would-be administrator had also to pass a searching medical test.

On acceptance into the service he was appointed to a particular colony with the rank of cadet, and would normally be posted to a District for training and experience. He served a probationary period of two years and, if he was regarded as satisfactory, would be confirmed in his appointment and promoted to the rank of Assistant District Officer. An essential pre-condition of the confirmation was that he had passed the higher tests in the official native language of his territory. In Tanganyika this language was Ki-suahili, generally known as Swahili. He also had to pass an examination in the criminal code applied to the territory.

Having crossed these hurdles our cadet served an average of eight years as an A.D.O. before being given the rank of District Officer. He was then qualified to take charge of a District if one were available, and received the local rank of District Commissioner. But in some of the larger and more important districts a D.C. might have one or more District Officers serving under him. This meant that the new District Officer might have to wait some time before advancing to the higher dignity of D.C.

As a D.C. his functions would vary according to the size and importance of his District. Those Districts that were more thickly populated, or which contained the Provincial Headquarters or an important coastal port or railway junction, would have a large staff of departmental officers, e.g. a medical officer, an agricultural officer, a magistrate, a veterinary officer, a public works engineer, or a superintendent of prisons. In Districts that were remote or sparsely populated, the D.C. would have to carry out many of the non-technical functions himself, and in all probability would have no Assistant District Officer.

Tanganyika covered an enormous area—more than 370,000 square miles—but its population was only about 6,500,000. Large stretches of the country were made uninhabitable by tsetse-fly and other pests. Such a country could not support large staffs of technicians and departmental officers in any but the most populous areas. Thus the D.C.s in the wilder regions carried a heavy load of work.

A D.C. in a District of this kind tried all court cases that were within his legal capacity as a magistrate. Sometimes the High Courts would add to his labours by giving him extended jurisdiction. He was responsible for the maintenance of his buildings and communications. For medical staff he might have an Asian sub-assistant surgeon (a term I shall not attempt to define) but more often an African tribal dresser whose training was limited to treating minor ailments or giving a few of the more simple injections. The D.C. was also responsible for the economic well-being of his Africans. He had to see that they planted enough food crops for their needs. He also had to assist them with advice as to the best means of earning the money to pay their taxes. This might take the form of encouraging them to plant cotton or coffee, or even—as I had to do—instruct them on preparing beeswax and extracting it from the hives of the wild bees. Again, he might find work for them on any nearby European plantations.

The D.C.'s principal function, however, was to act as political adviser to the tribal chief or chiefs within his district and to ensure the efficient running of the Native Administration. This particular duty involved supervising the administrative functions of the chief and the dispensing of justice in the tribal courts, and checking the finances of the native treasuries.

To carry out his duties towards the tribal chiefs and their administrations, the D.C. had to travel his entire district at least three times a year. In my early days there were no motor roads in Tanganyika except in the large towns, and all travelling had to be done on foot, with porters to carry the tent and loads for a journey of as many as ten days. For these 'safaris' the D.C. was granted an allowance of 8 shillings per night. In the days of retrenchment around 1930 this allowance was withdrawn and only the more dedicated men carried out the duty of touring their districts. Every officer in the service suffered a ten per cent deduction in pay during these hard times. The cuts made then were not restored when times became better.

Much of this travelling on foot had to be carried out in tsetse-infested country, and I have walked twenty miles in a day being bitten almost every yard. Fortunately this particular tsetse (*glossina morsitans*) did not carry sleeping sickness; however, it was fatal to cattle, and any stretch of country affected by it contained none and the population had to contrive other means of wealth.

If foot travel was at times irksome and uncomfortable, it had its political advantages. It meant that the D.C. became conversant with almost every inch of his District, and was in contact with most of its people. On the road he would meet travellers and talk to them, passing the time of day and gathering information about their activities and means of livelihood. In these wayside conversations he learned much about the affairs of the tribe and the conduct of the village headmen and other Native Authorities. He gathered more information when he pitched his tent for the night in the headman's village. After he had made a series of these journeys on foot the inhabitants would have got to know their white administrator and could talk freely to him. Many abuses might thus be brought to light, and the knowledge he acquired from these contacts with the ordinary men and women of the tribe was a useful background to his discussions with the chief and elders. When motor roads began to appear, as they did after a few years, these contacts were lessened: the traveller sped along in his car from one headman's village to the next. The chats by the wayside were lost, and the only contacts with the people were at the more formal gatherings in the precincts of the Native Courts.

After each tour the D.C. returned to his headquarters to find plenty of work awaiting him. Letters from Provincial Headquarters had to be answered, and reports written, and there were cases awaiting trial and numerous other administrative chores that had piled up during his absence. This at least was the fate of the D.C. who had no assistant white staff to relieve him of the donkey-work. He would have his small police force to inspect, and perhaps he would also have a small gaol containing minor offenders and persons sentenced by the Native Courts. He was responsible for the welfare of these prisoners, which meant ensuring that each got the daily scale of rations laid down by the prison authorities.

It will be seen that the District Commissioner had little time left over for relaxation. If he were the lone official on the station he could take an evening walk with a rifle or a shot-gun, but in the tropics darkness falls about 6 p.m. with little twilight beforehand, and he would be lucky if an hour's daylight remained after he had closed his office, so there was little time for outdoor play. In one of my districts I used to amuse myself by driving a tennis ball against the side wall of my bungalow. With the coming of darkness it was the custom to restore one's energies with a 'sundowner'. The evening meal followed at 7 p.m., and after that an early night. Every new working day began for us at 6 a.m.

In the lonely Districts, and these were numerous, officers would serve spells of a year or even two years without speaking their own language, except to themselves, or seeing another white man. Occasionally the Provincial Commissioner, the Superintendent of Police or some other official from Provincial Headquarters might come up on visits of two or three days—which not everyone welcomed. Many D.C.s regarded them as interruptions that upset the rhythm of duty: better to stick it out on one's own than suffer these well-meant intrusions. That, at least, was my own feeling. As long as our reports arrived regularly, headquarters concluded that all was well. A very small number of men broke under the strain of isolation, but the majority successfully completed their tour of duty. Some preferred this secluded life to the social amenities of the grander districts. All were dedicated to the interests of the African peoples committed to their charge.

2

INDIRECT RULE IN TANGANYIKA

Before proceeding to my narrative proper, I must touch on the system whereby we administered the African tribes of Tanganyika Territory. The Territory had originally been German East Africa, and after the First World War the mandate for its administration was entrusted by the League of Nations to Great Britain. The Germans had administered the African population up till their departure by what was known as the '*akida* system' which, for the time being we took over and applied.

The *akida* (an old African term for Governor) was a minor African administrator, each one with a prescribed area, who collected the native tax for the central government. He also ran a court for the trial of petty cases based on African customary law. His principal function, however, was to see that the orders of his German masters were obeyed. He dealt only with Africans.

When we took over, scarcely any trace of traditional tribal rule through chiefs and councils remained. The authority of the tribal chiefs had been stamped out after the Maji-Maji rebellion of 1905. This rebellion involved many of Tanganyika's tribes, and it raged with particular violence from the Kilwa region in the east to Songea and the shores of Lake Nyasa in the west. '*Maji*' means water: the witch doctors who incited the revolt assured the tribesmen that they had medicine powerful enough to turn the German bullets into water, and that when the Africans confronted the German forces, all they had to do was shout '*maji maji*' and they would suffer no harm. Although, needless to say, this charm did not work, many Germans had been massacred before the rebellion had been suppressed.

The German authorities took a terrible revenge. Every chief or senior headman, male or female, who had the remotest involvement with the rebellion was hanged. Near Songea I saw a huge mound several feet high which contained the bodies of some of the executed chiefs of the southern parts of the country. The Chief of Ifakara, where I was stationed in 1938, told me that his father, uncles and aunts had all been hanged, and he had only been spared because of his youth. Chiefs and headmen were not the only ones to suffer: a heavy toll was also taken of the ordinary Africans. It was generally accepted in my time that over 100,000 people had perished in the

14

southern part of the colony alone. The glut of corpses dumped in the bush was believed to be the reason why these parts had an exceptionally large quantity of man-eating lions and other carnivora for years afterwards. They were a serious problem in my time.

After this holocaust the Germans were clearly not prepared to leave any power in the hands of the surviving tribal chiefs: those who had had no part in the Maji-Maji or were too important to be deposed were stripped of any ruling or judicial authority they had previously possessed; they were allowed to retain only their titles. Their functions were taken over by the newly appointed *akidas*, and all administrative control was vested in the German commandants or administrative officers. This system, known as Direct Rule, was in operation until the arrival of Sir Donald Cameron as Governor in 1926.

Sir Donald had previously been Governor of Nigeria, and brought from there the system of native administration instituted by Lugard and perfected by himself, called Indirect Rule, otherwise rule through the tribal chiefs.

Within three years of Sir Donald's arrival, Indirect Rule was established throughout the Territory, wherever there was an identifiable tribe of sufficient strength in numbers, except in parts of the coastal belt where the population consisted of a hotch-potch of detribalised up-country Africans and half-caste Arabs and Indians. Where a tribal unit was identifiable but weak in numbers, it was encouraged to form a union with another tribe or other tribes. The ruling authority would be a council consisting of the chiefs of the tribes so unified, not a single chief. This kind of union could be achieved voluntarily only where the tribes were closely related by kinship and custom. In other cases it was considered essential to enforce it by administrative authority. Africans are not by nature co-operative outside their own tribes, but nevertheless most of the imposed unions were reasonably successful. In Bukoba, where I was briefly D.C. in 1943, the tribal authority—a council of nine chiefs— worked with the utmost harmony. It was sometimes discovered that an *akida* was himself the rightful chief, which meant that the Germans had been successfully hoodwinked.

The chief had power to appoint his own sub-chiefs and headmen. Each sub-chief governed a defined area and each headman, under the sub-chief, governed a group of villages.

Under African tribal custom, as in most tribal societies, chiefs, with their councils of elders, were the judges as well as the rulers of their people and before the Germans came to the country they exercised powers of life or death over their tribesmen. Obviously such extreme power had to be curtailed, and a system of tribal courts was therefore established. The chief's court was a 'First-Class Native Court'; those of his sub-chiefs were 'Second-Class'. In criminal matters jurisdiction was confined to simple crimes, also covering conduct insulting to the chief or defiance of his authority, with prison sentences in the first-class courts limited to six months and in the second-class to three months. Appeals lay from the second-class to the first-class courts and from the first-class courts to the court of the District Commissioner.

In ordinary matters of tribal custom or civil law, as between Africans, there was no limit of jurisdiction. Although every tribe had its own particular customs and laws, African society in the tribal areas did not generally make our distinction between civil and criminal law. To the African tribesman there is only one type of law, which has much more a civil than a criminal connotation, for all offences between Africans, even the offence of murder, could be atoned for or redeemed by payment in the currency of the particular tribe. This would be evident to anybody perusing the register of a chief's court.

In one case in which there was an appeal to me the man had charged his wife with assault. She had struck him on the head with an axe when his back was turned, but without hurting him seriously. It transpired at the hearing before the chief that the man had two wives, one elderly, the other young and comely. The elderly one was aggrieved that her husband was not giving her the amount of attention that was due to her by custom. He treated her complaint contemptuously and turned his back: provoked, the woman seized the first implement to hand, an axe. The chief ruled that the woman had been wrongfully treated and was within her rights in hitting back: far from taking her husband's part, he fined him. This was good tribal law, and I rejected the appeal. Of course, had the woman struck hard enough to kill her man, she would have been indicted for murder and the case brought in the first instance into my court, but as the blow was far from lethal, tribal law took its course.

The finance to cover the salaries of chiefs, sub-chiefs and officers of the tribal administration and other services was supplied from the tribal treasury, for which the main item of revenue was a share of the annual Hut and Poll Tax. Every able-bodied African thought to be over the age of sixteen was obliged to pay this tax. It varied from district to district according to the economic wealth or potential of the region, in some places being as low as 6s., in others as high as 15s., or 20s. In remote areas not easily accessible to markets the tax was at the lower figure; in other areas, where the Africans were coffee-growers or were rich in cattle or other forms of wealth, it was higher. There was also the Plural Wives Tax, which was simply an extension of the basic tax. An African paid an additional tax for every wife after the first. As each wife was entitled to a separate hut of her own, the reason for the term 'hut tax' becomes clear. Since a wife was of economic benefit to her husband, the purpose of the Plural Wives Tax was to spread the burden of taxation according to the individual's ability to pay. The missions disliked this tax, saying that if it did not actually encourage polygamy, it at least acknowledged its legality. But to have accepted this argument would have meant the well-to-do paying no more tax than the poor, an inequity which could in no circumstances be defended.

A quarter of the tax yield was remitted to the tribal treasury, which of course meant that treasuries varied in wealth according to the wealth of their tribal areas. Unavoidably some tribal chiefs were more highly paid than others. Where tax yield was low for natural and permanent causes and the tax rebate insufficient to keep the treasury in adequate funds, a grant-in-aid was supplied by the Central Government.

Other items of revenue accruing to the treasury were court fees and fines, licences of different kinds, market dues and such like. On the expenditure side were not only the salaries (of the chief and others) but the maintenance of tribal roads, court buildings and dressing stations, and other items that related to administration. At the beginning of every financial year the native treasury budget had to be drawn up, giving an estimate of current revenue and of expenditure for the year ahead. If funds permitted, items of non-recurrent or extraordinary expenditure could be included. These might be concerned with the construction of a new market, new tribal roads, reservoirs for cattle, court buildings, or other essentials. This budget had to be approved by the Provincial Commissioner before it could be put into effect. It had, however, to be supported by the D.C.'s recommendation before the P.C. would grant his fiat.

Administrative exercises such as the preparation of budgets were beyond the scope of most tribal authorities and nearly always the donkey-work had to be done by the D.C. himself; however, no budget was ever prepared without the chief being consulted and his agreement obtained. It was not the D.C.'s function to advance his own views as those of the tribe.

This new dispensation of Indirect Rule through the tribal chiefs and their councils was given legal effect by the Native Authority Ordinance passed in the Territory's Legislative Council. Under its terms the direct rule of the government through the District and Provincial Commissioners came to an end. The D.C. was now legally the adviser to the Native Authorities in his District. The advice which he tendered was tantamount to an order, but it was not so described: it was not good administration to force a Native Authority into a line of action to which it strongly objected, and the good administrator contrived that his advice should on the whole be willingly accepted. Direct orders were given to the authority only in exceptional circumstances. The Native Authority had power itself to frame orders and prescribe punishments for disobedience to them, but every order of this kind had to receive prior government approval.

By 1929 the system had been established throughout the Territory, except in the coastal areas where there were no cohesive tribal units. There was an initial difficulty in some tribal lands of finding the rightful hereditary chiefs. So effectively had the Germans suppressed the ruling families of the tribes that it was often difficult to decide who should occupy the 'royal' chair. Moreover, some of the individuals whose claim to the succession could not or would not be disputed were chary about coming forward, for they were old enough to remember the treatment their fathers and grandfathers had received at the hands of the former governing power. There were also numerous pretenders and not a few usurpers. While the ruling family could always be identified, the claims of its individual members to the chieftainship were often difficult to resolve. Different factions supported different individuals, and intrigue and witchcraft played their part in disputes between brothers and uncles; often these disputes dragged on for years after the Government had made its decision. It need hardly be said that a Native Authority subject to such intrigues suffered greatly in efficiency and in its ability to control its people.

Indirect Rule was undoubtedly the most equitable way of guiding African peoples in the management of their own affairs, giving them as much responsibility as they were fitted to bear. However, it had one serious weakness. The majority of the chiefs were either illiterate or of limited education. They were primitive and reactionary in their outlook and resistant to change. They were nearly all steeped in witchcraft, and usually the witch doctors were the powers behind the throne. This state of affairs could be tolerated if it were simply a matter of allowing the African to proceed along his time-honoured course of *laissez-faire* and stagnate in his unproductive village life, producing just enough for his daily needs and living perilously close to famine and starvation. But if we were to promote his economic and intellectual well-being by helping him to material progress and teaching him the advantages of education, then we would have to inject energy and initiative into the Native Authorities.

There were, of course, some chiefs who had received good basic education, mostly in the mission schools, and who were not without progressive ideas, and these could be trusted to put these ideas into practice with the friendly advice of the D.C. But most Native Authorities had to be led by the hand or pushed; and in the development of the natural resources of the District and the production of economic wealth for the tribe the D.C. was the real driving force. In cases where the hereditary chief proved inadequate, the D.C. himself was installed as the Native Authority.

It would have been unreasonable to expect that Africans, suppressed by the former colonising power and in many cases not far removed from the savage background of their forbears, could straightway adapt themselves to the demands of British administrative techniques. This fact was accepted. It was our task to make a beginning with the resources available, but with the long-term hope in mind that the descendants of the first Native Authorities would, with the benefit of education and example, be able to undertake functions and responsibilities that were rather too heavy for their predecessors.

There was another difficulty. The first Native Authorities or their predecessors had, in the far-off days before the arrival of the European, had complete control over the lives and property of their peoples. Any actions they took to acquire material goods were rarely questioned, and a tribesman's right against the acquisitiveness of his chief was non-existent. Atavistic practices of this kind had survived in many areas, and merged imperceptibly into the chief's prerogatives unless they were promptly checked. At times chiefs were not too particular in distinguishing between their property and the Government's, and D.C.s thus had to keep a close watch on tribal and government monies that passed through the Native Authorities' hands. Where this watch was relaxed there were cases of misappropriation, and in most of these severe action had to be taken. That the chief was the guilty party and received appropriate punishment did not protect the D.C. from having to take a heavy rap. More than once he suffered loss of promotion due to the dishonesty of his Native Authority.

An outstanding case in my time concerned a very important chief in Tabora, who had been regarded by the Government as a model Native Authority. This man misappropriated several thousand pounds of tax revenue. When charged he pleaded in extenuation that he had sixty wives to support and could not possibly manage to do this on his salary from the native treasury. Other chiefs carried out private tax collections of their own and pocketed the proceeds; no tax receipts were issued to the victims of these peculations. The gravity of this offence lay not only in its dishonesty but in the fact that if an African could not produce a tax receipt for a particular year he could be required to work on some public project, such as a road, unless he paid up. This meant double taxation for the victim, for he would rarely have the courage to expose the chief. It was therefore to be expected that the discovery of such an offence would merit the extreme punishment of deposition plus imprisonment. Other forms of misappropriation were the purloining of Native Court fees and fines.

My view in these matters was always that it was unfair to expose the chief or his staff to temptation over money by being careless in supervision or exercising no supervision at all. If a chief knew that any lapse on his part was certain to be discovered he would usually keep to the straight path. It was too easy to be censorious about these lapses, forgetting that chiefs who succumbed to temptation were acting according to a pattern of conduct that was acceptable in the ancient days of tribal government; nevertheless, for administrative reasons, these lapses had to be punished *pour Encourager les autres*.

Indirect Rule was not popular with educated Africans who had political ambitions. They saw it as a system designed by the ruling power to place the hereditary chiefs in an entrenched position and serve as a barrier to their own political advancement. They were unimpressed by the oft-repeated declarations of British governments that it was their established policy to prepare all African countries under their administration for self-government. How could self-government evolve from an organisation operated by reactionary and poorly educated tribal chiefs? The African who had gone through college or university would have no function in such an organisation, which was based upon the hereditary principle and the acceptance of tribalism. To the men who were campaigning for the independence of their countries heredity and tribalism were factors to be disowned. They could have no place in the new Africa.

3

KIBONDO

My service in the colonial empire began in 1923. The first three years were spent in satisfying my masters that I was a fit person to be confirmed in it. I had to learn the correct way of keeping District accounts and framing the annual estimates of revenue and expenditure, and I was responsible for the safe custody of government stocks and stores, which included Hut and Poll Tax receipt books.

My apprenticeship was at Tanga on the coast and my first chief was Philip Mitchell, whose local title was Senior Commissioner. Mitchell had been a district officer in Nyasaland (now Malawi) and had come to German East Africa with the King's African Rifles during the war. Like many officers of the British occupying forces he had joined the Tanganyika administration. However, as he was already a member of the Colonial Service, his posting to Tanganyika was really a transfer and not a new appointment. His career in the Service proved outstanding: he became at different times Governor of Uganda and of Kenya, and was High Commissioner of the Eastern Pacific before he retired. I learned much about administration from him.

I had one very disturbing experience during my time at the Tanga District Office. It concerned my custody of the tax books, each of which contained one hundred receipts in counterfoil, each receipt having the rate of tax printed on it. Tax books were held at the District Office and issued to the tax clerks when required. In Tanga at this time the rate of tax was six shillings, so that each tax book was equivalent in value to 600 shillings or £30. When tax was collected by the clerk he issued the original receipt to the payer and retained the counterfoil in the book for checking against his cash at the District Office; it was my duty to issue tax books to the clerks and check their cash returns bi-monthly. Late one evening, long after the office had been closed, a clerk reported at my bungalow with cash and tax books. These should have been lodged in the office safe overnight, but the key of the safe was held by the Senior Commissioner and I deemed it unwise to disturb him. So I put the books and cash in my own cupboard and locked it. The clerk departed, having first told me that he had been granted leave of absence from duty and would not be back at work for three weeks. The next morning, I went to the office for the daily stint, any thought of tax books absent from my mind. In the tropical heat a European's memory will sometimes play tricks, and the clerk, of course, was not there to remind me. A fortnight passed, and it was time to prepare the monthly returns of tax and other revenue for the Treasury at Dar-es-Salaam. My clerk and I then found we were several pounds short in tax books. We searched our minds as to which clerk had failed to report and might be planning a theft. At every turn we drew blank, and then suddenly the horrifying recollection came to me of the other clerk's call at my bungalow that night and of those tax books and cash lying in my cupboard. Quietly I left the office, went to the bungalow and unlocked the cupboard. Inside were the missing tax books and the bag of money. I brought them back to the office, explained to the clerk what had happened, and together we completed the return. If those books and cash had been found in my possession before I had had the opportunity of returning them, who would have believed my explanation? From this salutary experience I learned never to let government cash enter my private quarters.

In 1927, after returning from leave, I was given my first District—Kibondo, a remote outpost close to the Burundi border in Western Tanganyika. I was now an Assistant District Officer, with local rank of Acting District Commissioner. To reach Kibondo meant travelling on the Central Railway from Dar-es-Salaam to Kigoma and then marching 150 miles north on foot. Kigoma was the headquarters of the province of that name, and Kibondo was one of its Districts.

The route to Kibondo lay through Kasulu, another District of the province. Leakey, the D.C. at Kasulu, was away travelling when I passed through and I had to defer a meeting with him until later. From Kasulu to Kibondo was another 100 miles, more than half of this journey being through tsetse-fly belts; I therefore needed to traverse it as quickly as possible, marching by night as well as by day. There was no time for pitching tents or for long periods of sleep. A few hours' rest in the late evening was all that was possible. We would be on our feet again well before midnight and would march until six in the morning. After another few hours' rest we would be off again. My fifty bearers responded manfully, and we reached Kibondo in four days.

Our route lay across the Malagarasi river, which was the boundary between Kasulu and Kibondo. We crossed it in bark canoes and pitched camp on the opposite bank. We had now escaped from the last of the tsetse-fly belts, and we reached Kibondo on the following day.

I was met by the chief of the northern area, a young woman

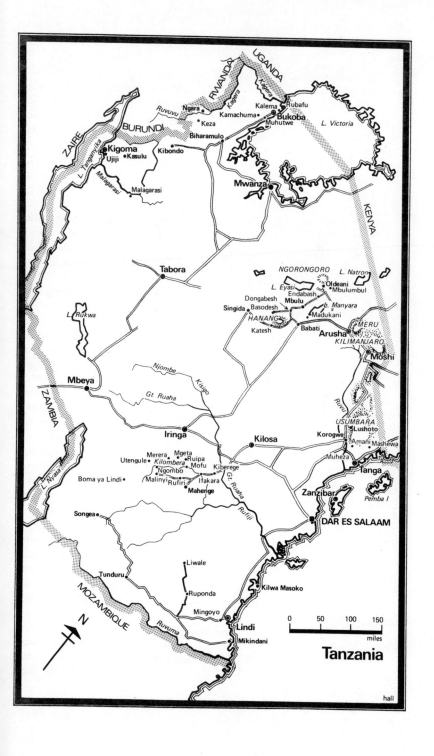

Tanzania

named Ruhaga. Her headquarters were within a mile of the District Office. Ruhaga was attended by a troupe of damsels whom she called her 'wives'. This was a fiction locally maintained when the chief was a female, and had no lesbian significance. These attendants fulfilled the function, to use a grandiloquent term, of ladies-in-waiting.

Women played a considerable part in the administration of Northern Kibondo. Of Ruhaga's sub-chiefs, whom I was later to meet, three were women. There were also some female 'headmen'. All these women ran their areas efficiently and were respected by their people. None of them was married; it was apparently contrary to custom for a female chief to marry, but it was permissible for her to have lovers, and her children were eligible to succeed her.

When I got to know Ruhaga better she told me that the village of Kibondo where she now lived was not the traditional seat of the chief. Her mother, also called Ruhaga, who had been chief before her, had moved to the present headquarters because she feared for her life and wanted to live near the District Office. It had not been the tribal custom for the chief to die naturally. Once when the elder Ruhaga was ill and the elders thought she might die, they sent two men to strangle her. She was quick to sense the purpose of their mission, but played for time by inviting them to have a drink. Her attendants, realising the situation, served her visitors with some strongly spiced beer, probably containing a potent drug, which reduced them to insensibility. Ruhaga escaped from the house with her attendants and fled to Kibondo, where she remained to the end of her natural life.

Her successor told me of another custom which was observed after the chief's death, and which might have had some connection with the ritual killing of the chief. The corpse was placed on an elevated frame of latticework. On the ground beneath it a fire was lit, and on the fire was placed an ox carcass already skinned and prepared for roasting. As the ox roasted the heat from the fire reached the corpse and caused its bodily oil and grease to drip into the roasting meat. When the meat was ready for eating its flesh was eaten by the chief's surviving relatives, including the heir to the chiefdom, and certain important elders of the tribe. This practice was called 'eating the chief'.

The only other chief in the Kibondo district ruled over the southern area. I kept no records of this period of my service and do not recall his name. One day I was resting in my quarters, and saw through the window a large procession in the midst of which a litter was being carried by bearers. Obviously the litter contained someone of importance. I made inquiries and learned that he was the southern chief, and that he was being taken to his camp down the road. Chiefs maintained camps of residence at District Headquarters for use when visiting the D.C. I went down to the camp to welcome the chief and found that he was gravely ill and unable to stand. I sat by his bed to give him what comfort I could, as I had no doctor to attend to him. The chief told me that his illness was the result of his brother's practising witchcraft on him. It was his belief that his brother hoped to usurp the chiefdom by killing him. The truth was that he was in the last stages of tuberculosis, but nothing would persuade him that his illness was natural. He stayed in the camp until he died, and I was helpless to do anything for him.

This was my first experience of the power of belief in witchcraft. Most Africans in my time were out of touch with modern medicine and attributed to witchcraft early deaths or any other untoward event, as well as any happenings that seemed to them contrary to nature, such as (in some tribes) the birth of twins, the birth of a child feet first or the birth of a deformed child. When they had made up their minds that witchcraft was being practised against them the first step was to identify the witch. They would soon persuade themselves that some family or individual with whom they were on bad terms was responsible. The next step was to think out the means of revenge. Sometimes they acted on their own, and this could mean murder; sometimes they invoked the assistance of a compliant witch doctor.

The dead chief had always been on bad terms with his brother, so that when illness struck him, his brother was held to blame. My recollection is that one of the dead man's sons succeeded to the chair, so that even if the brother had been guilty, his crime did not pay off. I was satisfied at the time that he was blameless.

Both chiefs were of Watussi origin, and it was my first meeting with that people. The Watussi are light-skinned with the sharp features found in those of Aryan stock. The men are tall, their average height being about six feet. Little is known of their origin. Ethnologists suggest that they came from the Caucasus region of Europe and moved by degrees down the centre of Africa centuries ago, conquering the various tribes on their way. There are men of their strain among the ruling clans in Uganda and eastern Zaire, but they are most in evidence in western Tanganyika, Ruanda and Burundi, where they have supplied the rulers of nearly every tribe. In my day they stood aloof from the people they ruled. Their role could perhaps be compared to that of the Norman invaders of England in that they became the overlords of the people they conquered. They maintained this dominance as long as European nations had control of Central Africa, but when the countries of this region became independent and African politicians took control their power disintegrated, and there have been wholesale massacres of Watussi in Burundi and Ruanda.

The Assistant District Officer who was looking after Kibondo until I arrived did not come to meet me. He was down with fever. When I went to his quarters to see him he was in a very low state. I told him of my meeting with Ruhaga. He warned me to be careful of her and suggested that she might try to seduce me. This assessment bore no relation to the truth: throughout my stay at Kibondo she behaved towards me with the strictest decorum and with a full sense of the dignity due to her position.

The Africans of Kibondo were of the Ha tribe. There were sections of the same tribe in Kasulu, but under other Watussi chiefs.

I must at this point give the reader a brief lesson in Bantu syntax, using the word 'Ha' as an example. U-ha is the country in which the Ha live. Ki-ha is the language they speak. Wa-ha means the men and women of the tribe. Mu-ha means one individual of the tribe. Strictly, the people of U-ha and Burundi, whose languages are related, would talk of Baha or Abaha and not of Wa-ha. The latter is the Swahili form.

I return to the Waha or Baha people. They were poor. One small Indian store in the village supplied their extra-tribal needs such as cloth and beads, and made barely enough to keep going. The people paid tax at the low rate of six shillings, but even that the individual had difficulty in finding.

The Waha were a neglected tribe. They were far off the beaten track, and no attempt had been made to teach them the cultivation of cash crops. Markets were far away, the nearest being at Malagarasi on the central railway line, a four days' journey on foot. What crops they grew were for their own food. There was no profit in taking these to Malagarasi, and in any case we discouraged Africans from depleting their food supplies by selling them for tax money. There were cattle in those parts of the district that were free from tsetse-fly, and some people raised their tax money by selling hides. However, the principal item of sale was beeswax. This had to be carried all the way to Malagarasi and sold to the Indian middlemen who frequented the market. An African would carry forty to sixty pounds at a time and realise anything from twenty to thirty shillings. Out of this he would pay his tax.

Parts of the country were thickly wooded and well stocked with bees. I therefore decided to concentrate my energies in the economic field on the production of beeswax. The Waha used barrel-shaped hives which were suspended from tree branches by bark rope; the hives were thus protected from marauding insects and badgers.

However, the recovery of the honey and wax was wasteful, since the greater part of the swarms was destroyed in the process of collection. To improve methods of collection I was given help by the Agricultural Department, who supplied queen-excluder zincs, circular in shape to conform to the design of the hives. I went through the country with a stock of these zincs attended by a Ha bee-doctor, in reality a witch doctor thought to have power over bees. We held meetings in every village and instructed people in the use of the zincs. Meanwhile, on my instructions, large numbers of hives were being made from tree bark. They were plugged at one end, with a small hole for entry and exit, and the excluder was fitted near the centre of the hive. When the time came for collecting the honey and wax, smoke would be used to drive the queen and the swarm into the chamber created by the excluder.

But first it was necessary to populate the hives with living bees. As a preliminary, a locally produced type of liquid sugar was poured into the hive; then it was our task to find the swarms. This proved remarkably easy, as we were operating at the swarming season, and we often found as many as five swarms in a day. The villages had their own intelligence system for locating swarms. The loading of the swarm into a hive was the most exciting part of the operation and here our bee-doctor gave ample evidence of his powers. The swarm was usually to be found hanging from the branch of a tree like a huge dark pumpkin. The doctor would approach it calmly and, smearing his forefinger with some kind of oleaginous medicament, its secret known only to himself, he would thrust it into the centre of this buzzing mass and with uncanny precision extract the queen. She would then be dropped into the hive, and the bees would be taken in his cupped hands and poured into the hive after her like handfuls of meal. Although normally chary of bees, I was too fascinated by this spectacle to be conscious of any fear. When every bee had been accounted for, the owner would seal the open end of the hive and hang it from a suitable branch at least 15 feet above ground.

This campaign continued day after day and village by village. With me and some African employees of the Agricultural Department, came a representative group of headmen, who were expected to propagate the new technique among their people. From this time on, at least during my time, money was voted annually in the native treasury budget to purchase queen-excluder zincs for free distribution to taxpayers.

In my travels through the District I could see that much of the country was fertile and suitable for coffee growing. The altitude in parts was 5,000 feet, the climate was cool and the rainfall adequate.

If I had had any doubts about this I had only to look across the Burundi border where Africans were growing coffee under Belgian tuition. So I decided to import at my own expense one hundred selected trees from the Belgian nurseries in Burundi. When they arrived I gave half to Ruhaga and distributed the rest among the more reliable sub-chiefs. The advantage of obtaining these particular trees was that they had been scientifically grown under the eye of experts in up-to-date nurseries, and proved in soil similar to that on our side of the border. I therefore had no hesitation in reporting my action to the Provincial Commissioner, thinking that I would get praised for my initiative. The contrary happened. A letter duly arrived from the Agriculture Department ordering me to uproot and destroy the trees: I had apparently committed an offence under the Plant Pests and Diseases Ordinance by importing plants into the Territory without a licence. That these coffee trees had been scientifically produced in a government nursery was not taken into account. As I had paid £30 for them I did not intend to lie down under this treatment. I asked for a retrospective licence on the ground that the trees were certified free from disease. This was refused, and the order to uproot and destroy the trees was repeated. I told Ruhaga what had happened and asked her to select a suitable piece of country well away from Kibondo for replanting her lot. The sub-chiefs who had the other trees were told to conceal them from alien eyes. When these precautions had been taken I reported to the Agriculture Department that the trees had been uprooted in compliance with their instructions.

This exasperating instance of officialdom taught me never to report too much to headquarters. Better to forgo the praise than risk the reverse. I would like to think that those coffee trees and their descendants are still proving a source of wealth to some Waha in Kibondo. If coffee is not being developed there these days on a large scale, a great opportunity for bringing prosperity to the area is being missed.

Four months after my arrival in Kibondo, I met Leakey by arrangement at our boundary on the Malagarasi river. It was our first meeting. I had heard tell that he was one of those rare people who had recovered from sleeping sickness, and that this had left its mark on him, but I found him cheerful and likeable, and we became great friends. At our meeting by the Malagarasi river Leakey and I decided that we should connect Kasulu and Kibondo by a motor road, each of us building the section on his own side of the boundary. Both sections had to pass through hilly country. I surveyed my line personally and kept the grades low, marking with stakes the exact course for the road to follow. The labour I employed were Waha who had defaulted on their tax payments. The law allowed me to requisition the labour of any able-bodied tax-defaulter for works of public importance. For every annual tax due, the defaulter had to work thirty days. Only age, ill-health or physical unfitness could excuse him. Without this tax labour I could not have constructed a road of this length, since the district vote would never have run to it. I have to confess that I did not press defaulters for their tax; their labour was of far greater value to me, and they too preferred it that way. If they had the money tucked away, they could keep it and spend it on other things. Besides I so arranged matters that I could employ them near to their villages, so that they could go home every evening. I thus assured myself a steady supply of labour for the three months that were needed to finish the job.

While collecting my labour force, I made a disturbing discovery. Ruhaga, who was not a woman of dynamic energy, employed an elderly Muha as her deputy to do most of her administrative work, including the supervision of tax collection. He was a kind of prime minister and wielded considerable authority. When tax-defaulters were brought before me to be registered for road work, many of them said that they had already paid their tax to Ruhaga's deputy, but had been given no receipt. When I investigated these charges, they proved true; for a long time this man had been defrauding the government of revenue. He was arrested and imprisoned and I warned Ruhaga that no more deputies were to be employed, and tax collection in future was to be the responsibility of herself and her sub-chiefs.

It was my ambition to be the first man to bring a motor-car into this part of Africa, and when Leakey reported that the road on his side of the Malagarasi had been completed, I made inquiries about buying one. I had heard through friends that an official going on leave from Tabora had a Standard Tourer for sale. I agreed a deal with the owner by post and, as I was due a fortnight's local leave, set out for Tabora to collect my purchase. Some months earlier I had acquired a Triumph motor-cycle, and used it for district travelling. I could negotiate the bush tracks on this machine, and with my servant sitting pillion I covered a lot of ground. It was the first internal combustion vehicle the Waha had seen, and while at first it aroused their curiosity, it did not make them gasp with wonder. They just shrugged their shoulders and said 'White man's magic!' There was nothing to be wondered at; the white man could do anything.

On this machine I set off for Tabora, with my servant behind me having sent my porters on ahead. We stayed three or four days on the Malagarasi bank while Waha dwellers near the river constructed dug-out canoes for the raft we would need to bring the new car across the river on our journey back. Dug-out canoes, made from hollowed tree trunks, are usually very stable in the water. When three dug-outs were ready we lashed them together with rough planking we had made from tree branches. This was our raft. To guide it across the river and withstand the strong current we threw a wire rope across and secured this to trees on either bank. A pulley to which a rope of bark was attached ran along this wire, and this rope was held by a member of the raft's crew when we were crossing. We tested the raft with my motor-cycle and all my loads that had been brought by the bearers. It carried them across safely.

So my servant and I, on the Triumph, set forth on Leakey's section of the road, leaving the porters to follow as fast as they could It was hard going, as Leakey's grades were much steeper than mine. We reached Kasulu and then Kigoma, where I found a purchaser for my Triumph. Then on by train to Tabora where I collected the Standard, and back again by train to Kigoma. Between Kigoma and Kasulu there was now a road of sorts, and I managed to bring the Standard through without mishap. From Kasulu to the Malagarasi it was not so good. Leakey's grades, which were tough going for a motor-cycle, were murder for a small tourer with a ten horsepower engine. The road went dead straight up and down the highest hills in Kasulu. However, with the aid of villagers on the way I managed to bring the Standard through to the Malagarasi.

It was early one afternoon when we reached the river. Two hours later raft and car with many of my possessions and my food supply had sunk out of sight in twenty feet of water. In midstream one of the canoes had sprung a leak and, with the force of the current, had filled rapidly with water and dragged the others down with it. We tried to pole the raft across, but the current was too strong and the river too deep for the poles to grip.

I would never make this mistake again but, alas, I had made it here, and the result was tragedy. A local helper was drowned. I had to swim frantically to the opposite bank in a river normally well stocked with crocodiles. My servant and another African clung to the wire rope that ran from bank to bank and we managed to rescue them with a bark canoe. We were now stranded in the bush forty miles from my headquarters without food or spare clothing, and what we wore was saturated. My servant and I spent the night in a disused, broken-down hut, hungry and sleepless. The vermin that abounded therein made sure that we had no rest.

The following day we set out on foot for Kibondo. I had a slight swelling in my groin, and the going was painful. After two nights in the bush we arrived at our destination. Our hunger had been relieved one night by a friendly African who roasted one of his chickens for us. Otherwise we had eaten nothing, although there had been water in plenty from the many streams that we crossed. By the time I reached my quarters the swelling in my groin had increased and I was hardly able to walk. There was nothing for it but to go to bed.

So had ended, ingloriously as I thought, my attempt to bring the first motor-car into Kibondo. The vehicle now lay, at a depth of twenty feet, on the bed of the Malagarasi. But one morning as I lay in bed my servant came into the room, grinning to tell me that the car had been salvaged. Some Waha living near the river, skilled swimmers, had by a fantastic feat of diving brought the car ashore by means of ropes made of tree bark tied to the front axle. Their technique had been to sink upright poles into the river bed close to the front wheels. They shinned down the poles with the ropes in their teeth and tied them to the axle. The only obvious damage suffered by the car was a broken glass in one of the front lamps. African witchcraft had been applied to keep crocodiles away while the divers were at work.

I had not the heart to tell the boy that the car's rescue had cost me a lot in insurance. I had now to be carried in a kind of litter, down to the river, where the car was standing on the bank apparently undamaged. We drained the engine and with paraffin oil washed its innards free of mud. We refilled the sump with fresh oil, washed out the petrol tank and refilled that with fresh petrol. We dried the magneto in the sun and refitted it, cleaned the sparking plugs, put fresh water in the radiator, turned the starting handle and the engine fired. We drove the car to Kibondo on our new road with its easy grades, but as soon as we arrived the engine stopped and could not be re-started. The engine gasket, I found, had been damaged by immersion in the river and water from the radiator was leaking into the cylinders. Until a new gasket could be fitted the car would not run again.

By this time my groin was so swollen and painful that I needed skilled medical treatment. I had already reported my condition, and I duly received instructions to travel to Mwanza on the south shore of Lake Victoria and report to the hospital there. To reach Mwanza I had to travel north to Biharamulo and from there to Bukoba on the lake, where a steamer could take me to my destination.

As I was now unable to walk any distance and my Standard was out of action, it was decided that I would sit in the car and be drawn by a team of Africans. As many of my loads as possible were put in the car and we set off on the journey to Biharamulo over non-existent roads. We had about eighty miles to cover, and made good progress until we came to a river thirty yards wide but fortunately not too deep. Here we stayed for three days while trees of sufficient length to span the river were felled. Men from nearby villages helped in this work. As manpower was our only lifting tackle I placed ranks of men on each side of a trunk, two men to every foot of length, and thus we levered each tree trunk across the water until the river was spanned. As there were four trunks to be placed there were four of these hazardous operations, and I sighed with relief when the last trunk had been put in position. I supervised this work sitting on the rear car cushions which had been placed on the river bank. Strong tree branches were placed crosswise on the tree trunks and these provided flooring for our improvised bridge on which the car was drawn across with myself at the wheel.

A few days later we reached Biharamulo, which boasted a cotton ginnery with a resident British engineer. The engineer got to work on my Standard and patched up the damaged gasket so effectively that the car was in running order by the time I was preparing to set out for Bukoba. Although still unable to walk I determined to risk driving it to the lake. We made the trip safely in one day on a passable road, although the distance was little short of a hundred miles. We were chugging through empty country with an uninspiring landscape and were descending one of many dreary hills when, as we turned the bend at the bottom, the broad waters of the great lake were spread below us. It was an unforgettable, beautiful sight.

I vaguely recall an uncomfortable journey in a rudely equipped steamer across the lake and a fortnight's stay in the European hospital at Mwanza. The Medical Officer was Irish, but that did not give him any cordial feelings towards me. He scoffed at my story that the groin swelling was the sequel to a frantic swim in a crocodile-infested river, and ascribed it to other less creditable causes. This diagnosis so angered me that I demanded another opinion. The Medical Officer of Health then examined me, and diagnosed haemorrhage of the small blood vessels in the area — and so it proved. This was a relief, because all along I had feared a rupture, which could only have been cured by an operation. The groin was drained and in a few days I felt well. My faithful Standard carried me safely back to Biharamulo, but I was not to see Kibondo again.

4

BUGUFI

Back in Biharamulo, the District Commissioner, Robert Maguire, greeted me with the news that I was posted to Bugufi, an area west of Biharamulo adjoining the Burundi and Ruanda borders. This place is now identifiable on the map by the name of Ngara.

Ruanda and Burundi, originally parts of German East Africa, had been awarded to Belgium as mandated territories after the First World War in acknowledgement of her part in the African campaign. When the Belgians had taken them over, some boundary adjustments were found necessary, and these resulted in Bugufi, originally part of Burundi, being returned to Tanganyika. This piece of country had not so far been administered and it was to be my task to organise the new administration. This would mean building a district office, a court building and living quarters for the administrative officer. Plans for these buildings had been prepared by the Public Works Department and were given to me by Maguire. As Bugufi would be a subordinate district of Biharamulo and I would have to account for my stewardship to its District Commissioner, I reverted to my substantive rank of Assistant District Officer. I was sorry to leave Kibondo and did not welcome a renewal of my solitary existence in a place totally unknown to me, but I had no choice.

I knew that Bugufi was divided into two sections by the Ruvuvu river, which rose in the Burundi hills and flowed north towards the Uganda border. South of the river lay the country of Chief Nkundabagore and north and west of it that of Chief Kinyamazinge. The Government had already sent some months ahead of me an African from Bukoba named Mapera s/o (son of) Kyaruze to act as adviser to Kinyamazinge, as this chief was known to be of low intelligence.

Armed with this slight knowledge I set forth from Biharamulo in the car. The rest of my loads followed on the heads of bearers. Maguire, or one of his predecessors, had built a quite good road as far as the Ruvuvu river, and by this I travelled, stopping for two days on the way at the headquarters of Chief Nkundabagore. He was tall, like most Watussi, and heavily built. But he was mild-mannered, and did not impress me as a man of dynamic energy or personality, and I suspected that he would find the new administration policy to be out of harmony with the habits of ease to which he and his predecessors had been accustomed. The old Watussi chiefs were satisfied if the people acknowledged their suzerainty by paying tribute and obeying their decrees. Otherwise they left their subjects to enjoy an easy-going way of life in peace. Under the new dispensation, more positive action was required of them — the economic development of their areas, closer attention to the finances of the native treasuries, and generally a deeper interest in their subjects' welfare.

These new duties were beyond the intellectual capacity of men like Nkundabagore. If there were to be progress and the tribesmen were to produce more and so improve their material condition, Nkundabagore and his kind could only be used as mouthpieces for the orders of the European administrative officer — although, as already pointed out, these orders would be described as advice and not as instructions.

It was this lack of initiative and intelligence in many chiefs that proved a serious weakness in the first days of Indirect Rule. Yet these backward and often illiterate potentates enjoyed the absolute loyalty of their peoples, so that with a chief who would accept the advice of the administrative officer in charge of the district, and assuming this advice to be sound, Indirect Rule worked for the benefit of the ordinary African husbandman.

When I first met Nkundabagore he had other matters than native administration on his mind. As behoved an important Mtussi chief, he had many wives. The chief was expected by the custom of the tribe to take a wife from each of the areas into which his country had by tradition been divided. While, in Nkundabagore's case, the senior wife who would produce his heir must be of the Watussi race, the offspring of the non-Tussi women would be carefully protected and enjoy the normal privileges that attached to a chief's descendants. Nkundabagore's present trouble was that he was ageing, and finding it difficult to play the full role of a husband to all his wives. This was a serious problem for any chief and a grave blow to his prestige. When Kasusura, a famous Mtussi chief in Biharamulo and proud father of 129 children, found that he was no longer capable of begetting progeny he took to his bed, turned his face to the wall and died. Nkundabagore had tried the medicines of his witch doctors, but these had proved of no avail. He was now anxious to try European remedies, if there were any such. Alas I was no doctor, and could not help him. I suggested that he should visit Bukoba where there was a British medical officer. I do not know whether he followed my advice, as he never discussed the question again. Many years later I was to learn that elderly gold miners on the Lupa river in southwestern Tanganyika recuperated their sexual powers with a diet of celery, and that every miner grew a celery patch in the garden of his hut. If I had known this at the time I might have recommended a similar course to Nkundabagore.

A few months after our first meeting Nkundabagore was to have further trouble on account of his women. He had decided to become a Christian and was baptised at one of the local missions. The mission authorities required that he part company with all his wives except one. He was sorely perplexed and sought my advice, but I refused to become involved. I confined myself to observing that dismissing his wives might be construed by his elders as a breach of that tribal law which required the chief to take a wife from every traditional area. This was a matter, I said, which he would have to settle with his tribal council, as it was quite beyond the scope of my brief as an administrative officer. In the end, I believe, he retained the youngest and prettiest of his Watussi spouses. This rearrangement of his domestic life did not affect the succession rights of the son already born to his senior wife.

The motor road to Bugufi ended at an escarpment above the Ruvuvu river — if ever we were to connect Bugufi with the outside world by motor road we would have a drop of more than 200 feet to negotiate. So for the time being we said farewell to the car, after raising it on blocks of wood and covering it as best we could. We went down on foot with our loads to the water's edge. The Ruvuvu at this point and throughout most of its length northward is a deep stream at least sixty yards across. It abounds with herds of hippopotami: wherever they are found there is deep water, for they like a depth of twenty feet or more in which to manoeuvre and exercise. They also like rivers with verges of thick vegetation or reeds, in which they can stable their young. They keep clear of frequented river crossings, and we could thus make a safe crossing in the inevitable bark canoes. On the Bugufi bank Chief Kinyamazinge, with a large crowd of retainers and Mapera, his adviser, awaited me. I was given the customary hand-clapping style of greeting, the meaning of which is 'Look, I have nothing in my hands; I come in friendship.'

Kinyamazinge, like his Watussi kinsmen, was a very tall man. He talked as if he had some vocal impediment and he did not look intelligent. Maguire had said of him that if he had had a little more intelligence, he could have been classed as a half-wit. I preferred to make my own judgment; I was sufficiently mature to know that first impressions can be misleading. Although I later found that Kinyamazinge had no great competence as a chief, he always co-operated loyally with me in putting my counsel into effect; and he had complete control over the Barundi tribe.

I took to Mapera s/o Kyaruzi at once, and appreciated his character and ability more the better I came to know him. He was highly intelligent and although his schooling had been limited to the local languages, which he wrote and spoke fluently, showed wide powers of judgment allied to a cool and well-balanced disposition. He was quietly spoken and had great gentleness of manner. He had also been thought highly of by the former German administrators, who had appointed him adviser to the Mtussi King of Ruanda.

My future headquarters (later to be called Ngara) were about twenty miles from the river, and we reached them the next day. They consisted of a wattle-and-daub hut with a compound containing other huts for my servants. I was to occupy this hut for the whole of my stewardship but there were compensations. The country between the river and Ngara and beyond was beautiful: broad rolling downs and hills stretched into the distance with a variety of colours produced by natural floral vegetation. Cattle grazed in the foothills—altogether it was a pleasing sight. And there were no tsetse-fly.

Until the hut was cleaned out and checked for snakes and other pests I decided to use my tent for sleeping. The hut I divided into two compartments with a wattle partition through which an opening gave access from one to the other. One compartment became my bedroom and the other my dining room. In the bedroom my camp-bed was placed alongside one wall, and beside it down the centre of the room a rope stretched from wall to wall, on which my clothes were hung. This screened my bed, and gave a measure of privacy.

In the dining room a square wooden box, part of my safari loads, served as a table, and the back seat of my car as a chair. With these primitive appointments I could eat in moderate comfort, but would be in difficulties if ever I had to entertain guests. However, I was not to be troubled with any for many months to come. Circumstances were to develop which would discourage the intrusion of visitors.

Before long I discovered that the hut was rat-infested. I heard the rats at night squealing and running over the floor and sometimes above my bed. My mosquito net kept the rats from my bed, but I did not want them in the room in case their fleas were infected with the plague. I decided to get a pair of dogs, and obtained two locally bred puppies. This was easy because the Barundi, like many other tribes, keep dogs for hunting. I was successful in domesticating these two animals, but far from hunting the rats, my dogs fraternised with them. Night after night as I lay in my bed with both dogs in the room I could hear the rats scampering at will over the floor free from any interference. Nevertheless I kept the dogs, because in this lonely place they were company of a sort.

Many months later, when the long drought to which I shall soon refer ended, the hut revealed other faults. Whenever there was rain it leaked like a sieve. I partly overcame this by buying a cowhide which was rain-proof, but unfortunately it encouraged insect pests, which dropped on to me at night through the mosquito netting. They had a nasty bite, and my chest was soon covered with sores. Our only medical service in Bugufi was a tribal dresser, and from him I obtained some antiseptic ointment. This kept the sores under control, but they did not disappear until I left.

When I was settled in, my first priority was to get my building programme going. African masons and carpenters had to be engaged and the ground for offices, court-house and living quarters chosen and marked out. Footings had to be dug and essential materials such as cement and lime brought in by bearers. There was no other form of transport.

The building material was to be sun-dried brick, for which we had to make our own moulds. In the hot sun the bricks dried quickly but the walls made of them had to be coated several times with lime-wash as otherwise they would have been porous. I was to have a long spell of hot, dry weather for my programme which was beneficial for me but had grave results for the tribesmen of Bugufi.

I decided to build the offices first and, after them, the court-house and a small prison. Since my instructions were to organise administration in the region, I needed a base from which to operate. Thus the offices had to come first and the living quarters last. When I left the district, the A.D.O.'s bungalow was still three months short of completion. Buildings made of sun-dried brick were classified as semi-permanent but, if the bricks had been properly made and dried, they could have a life of twenty years or more.

I did not know when I arrived at Bugufi that for nearly a year there had been continuous drought. The men we recruited as building labourers looked skinny and ill-nourished, but this was not uncommon in Africa, where most people existed on a subsistence diet. I knew these men would be well rationed while working for me. But as I was busy measuring out my future buildings, I was not to know that people were dying of hunger in the outlying villages and backwoods. After a few weeks, however, rumours of *njaa* (famine) began to reach me. Mapera confirmed them. Because of the long drought the crops had failed over a large area and there were no reserves of food. He advised that I should look into the matter, and I resolved to do so without delay.

Reporting the existence of a famine to Government can be risky. Famine relief is costly, and it was necessary to be sure of the facts before calling for it. It was therefore essential for me to make a thorough personal investigation.

Leaving the masons and carpenters to their work, I set out with Mapera and some of the Chief's representatives to travel round the country. I spent several weeks on this survey and found horrifying evidence of famine. In the bush we came across several bodies of people who had died grubbing for food. There were corpses in many of the small hamlets, and in one I counted four dead out of seven inhabitants. The other three were just sitting there in the final stages of starvation, almost too weak to move. To bury the dead was out of the question as nobody had the strength to wield a spade. All we could do was put all the corpses in a hut and set it on fire. Such mass cremations were the only way of keeping down disease.

Not all the victims, we discovered, belonged to Bugufi. The drought and accompanying famine had spread over Burundi and Ruanda even more savagely, and starving tribesmen were coming to our side for food, although the Belgian Government was beginning to organise its own relief. Official estimates published after the famine put the casualties at more than 50,000. Our share of these was about 2,000.

Wherever Mapera and I travelled we found evidence of hunger and death. But for the few herds of cattle and their supplies of milk the death toll would have been still higher. I gave orders that all the milk available should be reserved for the children. The pictures published many years later of starving children in Biafra reminded me of the children of Bugufi in those harrowing days—the same swollen stomachs, matchstick legs, ribs sticking out of little pinched chests and lacklustre eyes.

I could no longer hesitate to report that famine existed on a large scale, and sent runners to Biharamulo with a request for urgent supplies of maize and other foods sufficient for at least 10,000 starving people. Bugufi north of the Ruvuvu had a population of about 26,000 and I reckoned that more than one-third were affected by the famine. As the food had to come from Lake Victoria and loads would have to be carried by head bearers over a distance of 120 miles, deliveries would take nearly a fortnight. We would have to wait patiently. During this period of waiting, advised by Mapera, I arranged four points of distribution and erected storage barns at each, the object being to save the hunger-stricken people the strain of travelling long distances. One of these barns was at my head-quarters. Eventually the first deliveries arrived, all the way from Mwanza. They had been carried across the lake to Bukoba and thence on foot. There followed a steady stream of supplies until I was able to give the all-clear four months later.

Unfortunately the first lot of food consisted entirely of rice, a diet completely foreign to the Barundi of these parts. Maize was not yet available. It would have been dangerous for people with their stomachs distended by hunger to eat this rice in its granular form, so at each distribution centre I had to employ women to grind it into meal. These women were put on a special ration, as they too were among the famine sufferers. Distribution was rationed on a weekly basis, so that stocks could be used with moderation and not prematurely consumed. As the weeks rolled by, stocks of maize arrived and took the place of rice. We were concerned with feeding the mothers, the children and the elderly. Most of the young men had left for places where there was work and food. They had in fact deserted their families but this on the whole was good because they could have done little by staying, and their absence reduced the numbers of mouths to feed. Although the Belgians were operating their own relief across the border, many of their people slipped to our side to be fed. These intruders were soon detected and sent back. Every available pound of food had to be reserved for our own people.

A famine usually produces unpleasant incidents, ours being no exception. The store barns at the distribution centres were subject to raiding and had to be guarded by African police from my own staff, aided by the Chief's own guards.

We once had an unusual raid. It was my practice to carry out routine inspections of the centres, and one night I was encamped at one of them when it was visited by a herd of elephants. This was my first encounter with elephants in Bugufi, and indeed my first intimation that we had any in the district. I was asleep in my tent when the guards raised the alarm. The elephants were smashing down the storage barns. Cereals were their favourite diet, and they had somehow discovered the existence of our maize-filled containers. I sprang from my bed, grabbed the .303 sporting rifle that I always kept under my bed, and, wearing only my pyjamas, dashed out of the tent. In the darkness I could hear the crashing noise of the barn being demolished but it was a very dark night (another indication of the elephants' shrewdness) and against the dim skyline I could only just make out the vague silhouettes of these huge animals. To judge from the noise, a fair number of them were raiding our precious rations, and the nearest was only about ten yards from me. There was nothing for it but to take a chance shot in the dark towards the source of the noise. I fired two shots rapidly and waited. The noise of smashing and crashing stopped suddenly but

I could hear nothing else. I waited for about ten minutes and then cautiously lit a lamp. There was no sign of any elephants, but our barn was wrecked. However, very little of the maize and rice had been touched. Elephants, even in large numbers, can move quietly, and these had gone without a sound.

I went back to bed. As I was at breakfast, in the morning, a Murundi tribesman reported a dead female elephant half an hour's walk from my camp. My shots had been more effective than I thought. The wrecked barn was restored in a few days, some of the scattered grain was rebagged and distribution continued as before. Elephants gave us no further trouble.

Another day when I was at my headquarters a Murundi, pursued by an angry crowd, ran to me as I stood at the door of my hut. He was bleeding profusely from the head and both his ears had been cut off. Before he could complain to me his pursuers arrived and told me that he had been caught stealing food from a hut. In times of famine this was the most serious crime that a tribesman could commit Whereas murder could be atoned for by the payment of blood money, theft of food in times of scarcity was punished under tribal law by death. I told the thief that he was lucky to have got away with his life and that if I had not been there he would probably have been killed. To have taken this case myself and punished the thief's attackers under English law at a time like this would have been extremely unpopular and indeed a mistake. I sent the thief and his accusers to the Chief's court.

The Barundi method of execution for stealing food was impalement, a form used by most African tribes. Some months after this incident a Roman Catholic missionary who had grown old in mission service showed me photographs of an execution that he had been unable to stop. The sight almost made me sick.

One evening during the height of the famine I decided to visit a distribution centre near the Ruvuvu. I set out in the early afternoon, leaving behind my head servant with instructions to sleep in my hut and guard my few possessions. The following morning he came to my camp, in a state of panic. His first words to me were 'I have killed a man', and he told me that he had been sleeping in my bedroom when a noise awoke him. A lamp with wick turned low gave sufficient light for him to see two men in the room, armed with spears, but he was lying against the wall in shadow and they did not see him; otherwise he might have been killed. One of these men drew aside the screen of clothes beside my bed and raised his spear, thinking that I was in the bed. My servant, as soon as he took in the scene, sprang to his feet, and the men, taken by surprise, raced out of the hut. He chased and caught one of them and pummelled him until he fell. When the man made no attempt to rise he looked at him and found he was dead.

I commended my servant for his courage, and told him to return to Ngara and have the corpse buried. In other circumstances he would have been indicted for manslaughter, but it was not the time or the place for legal formalities. It turned out that the two would-be assassins were starving Barundi from across the border. They had been seen that afternoon lurking near the food store at my camp and had no doubt decided that if they could kill me they would be able to make a sufficient haul of food for their future needs. From that day onwards I had a police guard at my hut.

An unusual aftermath of this famine was a plague of man-eating leopards. Their appearance was almost certainly due to the multiplicity of unburied corpses in the Bugufi countryside. Like the lions who frequented south Tanganyika after the *Maji-Maji* rebellion, these leopards fed on human flesh and found that they liked it. We identified four of them, male and female with fully grown cubs, and eventually trapped them all.

One night I was aroused from sleep by the barking of my dogs, which were in the room with me. I awoke to find a leopard peering into the bedroom and sprang from the bed, grabbing my rifle which was always handy, but the animal was too quick for me and escaped.

This incident made me decide to build a trap in my compound: a small but strong stockade with a narrow entrance. A goat was placed in the stockade as a bait. To reach the goat the leopard would have to pass through the narrow passageway that led to the stockade. Its head would press against a web of cord which was attached to the trigger of a rifle mounted on a frame above and pointing downwards, at the back of the animal's head. We killed all four in this way.

Late one night I heard the goat bleating, and seconds later came the shot. In the morning we found the leopard, a young male, dead in its tracks. Perhaps suspecting the trap, it had tried to get at the goat through the wall of the stockade. It had managed to get its claws into the goat's skin and tear it away, but the wall of the stockade was too strong for it and it had decided to go in through the passageway. We patched up the goat and it soon recovered from its wound.

Some days after the death of the first leopard a woman was killed in a village five or six miles away. We built a trap in this village and used the same goat as bait. Two nights later this trap gave us our second leopard. We had to wait for another killing before trapping our third leopard. Meanwhile villagers in different parts of the country were in danger, but before we could build a trap we had to be sure that one or both of the surviving beasts was concentrating on a particular neighbourhood, and not hunting at random. At last we heard that this leopard had tried to tear down the door of a hut, and we built a trap in the village. Within days we had our third leopard.

There now remained only one more, the father of the brood. It was some weeks before we heard that in a village near the river it had killed three men and left one half eaten, all in one night. We hastened to this village and built our trap, again using the goat as bait. The leopard returned the same night but ignored the goat; it appeared that only human flesh would satisfy it. So the following night we adopted the gruesome method of putting the half-eaten corpse in the trap. That night the leopard returned, but evidently suspected the trap and went away. Meanwhile all the villagers had been warned to stay indoors after dark. The next night the leopard returned and again ignored the trap. After it had tried unsuccessfully to break into a hut, the smell of rotting human flesh overcame caution, and it went to its doom in the entrance to the trap. Even then the rifle bullet only inflicted a disabling wound, and an African policeman and I had to finish the leopard off with our rifles. With the death of this fourth leopard the misfortunes of the Barundi arising out of their famine could be said to have ended.

We had fed over 10,000 people. There now remained the work of rehabilitating them and restoring their seed supplies. All that we had achieved so far was the rescue of the community from famine, but they were completely without reserves of seed for future crops.

There should never have been famine in this fertile land, in spite of the lack of rain. It abounded in rich valleys well supplied with water that seeped through the hills from the riverine complex surrounding Bugufi. Much of this water came from the Ruvuvu and its minor streams. The valleys had never been cultivated, and were overgrown with vegetation. The choice of one of them for our seed garden was obvious, and I soon had evidence of what a communal effort could achieve. Two hundred tribesmen were collected, put on full rations, and set to the work of clearing about ten acres. In a few weeks the vegetation was cleared and irrigation furrows were dug. I had ten hundredweight of maize-seed ready for planting, and if in time ,it all matured we would have made a good beginning. But who was to plant it? To these Africans women symbolised fertility, and if seed was to grow it was they who must be the sowers. So a large company of matrons was assembled, to the delight of several hundred onlookers, and in a few days all the cultivated ground had received its precious burden. Three months later I stood on the high ground above the valley and looked down upon a great harvest of ripening maize. I knew that the famine was finally at an end.

By now the people were strong enough to resume cultivation on a full scale, and Chief Kinyamazinge gave orders that every valley was to be cleared and planted with crops—sweet potatos, cassava, beans and other safeguards against hunger. I asked the Chief why these valleys had never been used before and he answered that the witch-doctors had advised him that bad luck would befall the tribe if the valleys were cleared, because the evil spirits that dwelt there would not take kindly to being disturbed. The same witch-doctors had assured him that they would supply all the rain necessary for crop production on the land used in the past.

Here again was an example of how witchcraft dominated the lives of chiefs and people. The witch-doctors' profits from their profession as official rain-makers would have been depleted if it were proved that food could be grown under irrigation in the valley without mishap to the cultivators. When in later months I saw these valleys teeming with food I wondered if this exposure of their false teachings might finally and effectively destroy their malevolent influence. Time alone could supply the answer.

My energies and attention were so taken up with famine relief during the first months in Bugufi that I had little time to study other aspects of the environment. In the course of my travels to investigate the food situation I came across pygmies for the first and only time near Lake Burigi, in thick forest country on the eastern side of the district. I was walking through this forest one morning with Mapera and my Barundi escort when we met a party of about ten men and women, all less than five feet tall. I stopped and attempted to have speech with them. They spoke a language different from Kirundi, but some of the Barundi with me knew their language slightly and through these interpreters I managed to converse after a fashion. It was not enlightening and consisted mostly of such basic questions as 'Where do you come from?', 'Where are you going?', 'What do you eat?', and so on. They lived in the depths of the Burigi forest and subsisted on what nature provided—fish from the lake, small animalia and even snakes from the forest and the wild spinach and tomatoes that grew in these remote parts. The men carried bows and arrows, and I guessed that they indulged in some game poaching. They did not practise cultivation, and so could never be troubled by the fear of famine. I could not speculate on the size of their community, or even whether they lived in a community at all and not as individual family units. As far as I knew they had never paid taxes, but it was clear that they did not ask for any service from the Native Authority and were content to live their secluded life in the forest. They obviously used no money and their scant clothing consisted only of bark cloth. They had a distinctive woody smell derived, I supposed, from their environment and from the garb they wore. To have taxed them or required labour instead of tax would have been quite wrong; had they been taken from their forest environment their health and even their lives would have been endangered. I decided that they must be left in peace.

Stanley and other old explorers tell how African villagers fled into the bush at the approach of white-faced strangers. I experienced this as we travelled further north and west towards the Ruanda border. Here there was some very wild country, and it was clear that no white administrator, German or other , had ever visited it. In the depths of this unfriendly bush I found a collection of huts but no sign of life. At first I thought that the village had been abandoned because of the famine. We sat down in the clear space in front of the huts and rested, but looking round we spied a small face peering at us from behind a tree. I called out to the child and beckoned; very cautiously a small boy came forward. Mapera spoke to him in Kirundi and gradually he lost his fear. I am sure that he was being used as a stalking horse by the other villagers who were lying hiding in the nearby jungle. When they saw that no harm came to the child from this strange person with the white face, they came out one by one and greeted us. From our talk with them I learned that I was the first white man (*omuzungu*) they had ever seen. They all looked woefully hungry, but told us that they had partly made up for the loss of their crops by trapping fish and birds. No doubt they also tried trapping some game; but this was no time to think about game laws. In times of famine in Africa people who lived closest to the jungle always came off best. In the jungle itself were the wild fruits and vegetables, and the game that could sustain life. Hundreds if not thousands kept themselves alive through the bounty of wild nature.

When the famine was almost at an end, my thoughts had to turn to roads and communications. Bugufi's isolation from the outside world had to be ended. There could be no question of large-scale tax collection, for few people had any money. The wages of each worker would be a tax-exemption ticket for a thirty days' stint. I could thus recruit enough men to complete the road-building project.

First a complete survey of the route from the Ruvuvu to Ngara had to be made, and the escarpment on the Biharamulo side of the river needed to be negotiated. I tackled the escarpment first. As we had no surveying instruments and would not have known how to use them anyway, we could only rely on eyesight. On the Bugufi side of the river there was high ground from which we had a bird's-eye view of the hilly ground on the far bank. I pointed out to Mapera and the attendant Barundi how the road would have to run, winding to and fro down the hill in a gradual descent, to achieve a gradient suitable for motor vehicles.

After I had pointed out from our eminence the route that our road to the river should take, my Barundi companions, with their wonderful sense of locality, were able to identify its exact course on the ground when we crossed the river to survey the escarpment. It remained only to check in detail each terrace of the road for gradient as we went along. In one week we had finished the job using a method that was primitive but effective. Men carrying white flags mounted on poles were sent about a hundred yards ahead from each point; if the flag bearer seemed to be on too steep a grade we waved him down to what our eyes told us was viable. Mapera and I then assumed the role of elephants, slowly walking the distance to the flag. If the going was easy we drove in a stake every five yards; if it became difficult we stopped and waved the flag-bearer down lower, and then resumed our walk and our stake-pegging until we reached the flag. We reasoned that if the gradient was easy for the walker, it would be easy for the motor-car. This we repeated first in one direction and then back again, moving upwards. On the way we had to mark out the radius of each of the many bends. This work demanded extreme accuracy, for even a car with a long wheelbase should be able to negotiate every bend easily and safely. When the survey was completed, the escarpment section measured about a mile and a half with no gradient of more than one in seventeen. When our survey reached the top we found we were a quarter of a mile from the Biharamulo road and the place where 'the great car' had reposed all these months.

A car would have to travel a mile and three-quarters to ascend or descend 300 feet. The easier the gradient on tropical soil the less is the erosion from rain and flood and hence the cost of upkeep. A steep gradient, even if within the capacity of a motor vehicle, means deep washaways after rain unless the track can be metalled, something which was not feasible in Bugufi then.

Having completed our survey of the escarpment, we now had to tackle the route from the Ruvuvu to Ngara. This presented no serious problems, and, using our white flag technique, we accomplished it in a few days. I left the construction of this section to an African overseer while I concentrated on the escarpment section. I pitched a tent by the river and lived there for nearly two months, paying occasional visits to my headquarters.

While the road work was going on, the raft that was to bring cars across the river had to be built. This time we decided to use six dug-out canoes, not four as on the Malagarasi, and so six tall trees had to be felled. The Barundi were experts at making dug-outs, and inside five weeks all six trees had been hollowed out and shorn of their bark. They were then turned over and the outsides treated with boiling tar to seal them and make them rot-proof. After drying in the sun for a week they were launched in the river and decked with cross-beams made from heavy tree branches and secured with bark rope. To give a smooth run-on for cars, strips of galvanised iron were laid lengthwise along the deck. The completed raft at this stage had freeboard of about four inches. By the time the escarpment road was ready for use, the freeboard had increased to more than a foot thanks to a hot sun that speeded the drying-out.

Almost four months to the day after we had started work the entire roadway was finished and the raft ready for testing. Would the Standard engine run after so many months of inactivity? After a little persuasion it did, and I drove it safely down to the river. On each bank we had prepared concrete landing stages for the loading and off-loading of cars. As the Barundi knew nothing about mixing cement and concrete I had to do most of this at first, but by degrees they learnt this strenuous art and became quite expert at it. The car was run on to the raft on planks laid from the landing stage to the galvanised iron deck.

Next was the problem of bringing the raft across the Ruvuvu. The river was broad and deep, and flowed silently with a strong if sluggish current. I had learnt from the Malagarasi disaster not to rely on propulsion by poles, so we adopted a new technique which depended on strong ropes and manpower. Four pieces of heavy bark rope were prepared, the length of each exceeding the width of the river. Two were tied to the front and two to the stern of the raft. The front pieces were handled by men on the Bugufi bank, whose job was to tow; the stern pieces were held by men on the Biharamulo bank, whose job was to hold the raft against the current. I then mounted the raft and gave the go-ahead. We crossed safely.

While we were making all these preparations the Agricultural Officer arrived from Biharamulo. He had learnt from my reports to Maguire that the road across the river was near to completion. After the Standard had been taken across and the raft returned to the other bank he bravely loaded his car and came across after me. We then drove without mishap to Ngara, a journey of about twenty-five miles which nonetheless took us over two hours to complete. As we pulled up before my hut that night, I reflected that in the ten months of my stay there a famine of considerable proportions had been tackled and Bugufi opened to the motor-car. We celebrated with a drink.

A week or two later Chief Kinyamazinge decided that he too must have a motor-car. On the day when it was to make the river crossing, I heard that he was very drunk, and I kept out of the way so as not to embarrass him. No doubt he was celebrating what for him was an historic event.

By this time it was safe to report to Maguire that he could make the full journey to Bugufi by car, and he soon came to visit me, attended by no less a person than our own chief—the Provincial Commissioner from Bukoba. They brought with them a motor lorry, the first commercial vehicle to enter the district. The raft was capable of carrying the heaviest vehicle on the roads, and before I left Bugufi many lorries were to come in to collect and take away local produce for export. The days of transport by head-bearer were at an end. Should there ever be another famine, relief would come quickly.

I continued the existing highway, with Mapera's help, to the Burundi border, and I drove along it several times to meet my neighbour, the Belgian commandant. This road is still in use and has become the main highway from western Tanzania into Burundi.

Maguire and the Provincial Commissioner stayed for a few days to discuss local problems and inspect the progress of my buildings. The offices and courthouse were not yet complete, so we had to hold our discussions in my wattle-and-daub hut. On the day of their departure I escorted them to the river and saw them safely across. I was not sorry to see them go. There was nothing personal in this feeling: I was pleased to see the occasional visitor, provided he did not stay too long. After two or three days I was quite happy to see him depart, leaving me to my own company. Visits seemed to break the rhythm of existence. I was glad of the temporary pause from my labours which they gave me, but the enjoyment was always quickly exhausted, and all I then wanted was to get back to my self-imposed routine. This reaction could have been due to overwork —indeed I was subconsciously aware of this. Men who have served on lonely stations in Africa have either worked a very long day or taken to drink. My working day lasted at least twelve hours, and it was never before eight o'clock in the evening that I called a halt. This intensive concentration on work rejects lengthy interruptions from the outside world—and it cannot be maintained indefinitely. The breaking-point has inevitably to come: mine was still some months away.

About thirteen months after my arrival the offices and courthouse were ready. The office building had four rooms, to allow stores accommodation, as well as staff. The courthouse was a simple structure consisting of one room only. It was built separately from the offices in order to give it a special distinction. It was the Hall of Justice where the majesty of the law was upheld, as distinct from the District Office where day-to-day business was transacted. We had a ceremonial opening, with the Chief and elders in attendance.

I now had more time to pursue my normal administrative duties, visiting the sub-chiefs' areas and making routine inspections of the tribal courts. I crossed the river and called on Chief Nkundabagore. His people had not been affected by the famine and I had therefore not so far given them much attention. I tried to make up for this neglect; nevertheless, the area north of the river continued to be my major interest, and this I covered intensively.

I would pick up strange and valuable information travelling around African villages. A fact of outstanding significance which I learned, and which the tribal dresser confirmed, was that venereal disease did not exist among the Barundi ruled by Chief Kinyamazinge. The reason was that sexual promiscuity was severely discouraged by tribal law and custom, as I discovered from the chief's court register. There was a case of adultery committed with an unmarried girl. Punishment for the crime was inflicted not on the offenders themselves but on their fathers, both of whom were heavily fined. The chief informed me that in earlier times, before the coming of the Europeans, the girl and her lover would have been executed. Since such punishment was no longer feasible, he thought it just to hold the male parents of the offenders responsible.

The principle underlying the infliction of death as a punishment in Kirundi law was that every individual who was a menace to the stability and unity of the tribe should be permanently removed. This would apply to those who breached the marriage laws or who stole food in times of scarcity, but not to the killer. Murder was an inter-family affair and could be compensated for by retribution in kind. To slay the killer was to weaken the manpower of the tribe, which would lose two of its number instead of one.

During this period I carried out some amateur geographical surveying with the aid of a measuring wheel and prismatic compass, and made a map of the locality. Detailed maps scarcely existed and I hoped that my efforts would be of use to future officers when they planned their inspection tours.

At this time I had a serious quarrel with the Lutheran Mission. At the height of the famine, this mission had applied for leave to establish a church in Kinyamazinge's territory. I was in no mood to encourage applications of this kind when people were suffering acutely from hunger. However I observed strict protocol by referring the matter to the chief, because no mission could enter any tribal territory without the Native Authority's sanction. I advised Kinyamazinge, as I was bound to do, that the introduction of a mission could cause many complications. There would be conflict between tribal law and mission teaching, and since the Chief and many of his elders practised polygamy they might find themselves in conflict with the missionaries. Moreover the mission would require land, of which there was little to spare, and what there was would be required for the increased agricultural developments that were then being encouraged. Any allocation of this land to missionaries would not be popular.

Kinyamazinge turned down the Lutheran application; whereupon the head of the mission sought an interview with the Governor in Dar-es-Salaam and accused me of deliberately blocking his effort to bring Christianity to the Barundi. The Governor gave him short shrift, and that was the end of the matter as far as I was concerned. But some years later a second application was successful, and I wondered if on the later occasion the views of the Chief had been clearly and thoroughly ascertained.

I always had mixed feelings about the impact of mission teaching on tribal institutions. There is no doubt that some Christian doctrines, however great their ethical value, undermine the social customs of a tribe. Polygamy, for example, contrives that every woman has a husband and family of her own. This is important in societies where, under normal conditions, as proved by census returns, females outnumber males by ten or eleven per cent. Monogamy creates the surplus woman, who in the environment created by mission activity usually turns to prostitution, the gateway to venereal disease. In Bugufi there were no missions, but tribal discipline was vigorous. In Bukoba, about 120 miles away, there were many Christian missions, many so-called African Christians—and a high rate of venereal disease. Prostitution was much in evidence. Is it unfair to blame the missions for this state of affairs?

This was not the time to promote development of cash crops in Bugufi. The famine was too recent, and reserves of seed for future harvests were far from adequate. The ten communally planted acres of maize could only make a token contribution to the problem. It would take many months of food production to bring back the community to a proper standard of nutrition. Such money-earning crops as coffee and cotton would have to wait for other seasons, and another factor was that I no longer had the energy to embark on new ventures. After the past eighteen months, added to my spell in Kibondo, I was near the point of mental and physical exhaustion.

The decline was hastened by a severe attack of malaria. From this I recovered after six or seven days in bed, as most of us do, but the fact that I was many days' journey away from skilled medical treatment and had only my servants to nurse me left me acutely depressed. I became restless: if I went to my office in the morning I could not sit at my desk for more than a few minutes, but had to be up again, even if it meant wandering around aimlessly. Another effect of my illness was complete loss of appetite and a growing belief that my health was rapidly degenerating. From this it was a short step to heavy drinking, yet I was never intoxicated: alcohol did not give me the mental black-out that I sought but, on the contrary, intensified my introspection. I ate hardly anything and began to suffer from acute insomnia.

At this time I had been asked by the Government to write a report on the land laws of the Barundi tribe. As I had lost all my powers of concentration, the report that I managed with desperate effort to compile was poor and did my reputation little good. Clearly I was in no state to administer the district, and as my nervous condition grew ever worse, I wrote to Maguire asking to be relieved. Permission was promptly granted and I was told that I might go before my relief arrived; I shall always be grateful to Maguire for his understanding. In the compound of my hut I had dug an inspection pit for the Standard. I filled it in while waiting for Maguire's reply to my application for leave: it looked too much like a grave.

The posting of men to lonely outposts was a problem that caused great concern to the Tanganyika Government. The medical authorities were strongly opposed to long-term tours; on the other hand, to relieve men at short intervals raised staff difficulties, and it was reckoned to be bad administrative policy to subject Native Authorities to frequent changes of the officers sent to advise them.

On the day I left, Kinyamazinge and Mapera escorted me to the Ruvuvu and there bade me good-bye. After the eighteen months of our friendship and co-operation, we took leave of each other with deep regret. I crossed the river for the last time and reached Biharamulo in the old Standard the same evening. Maguire was kindness itself: until we met he had not realised how rundown I was. The sight of another white man was a salve to my worn nerves and I enjoyed my few days' rest at his headquarters before going on to Bukoba *en route* for home. At Bukoba I parted with 'the great car', selling it to a local Indian merchant for £35. It had served me well.

5

THE SOURCE OF THE NILE

I have already mentioned my interest in map-making and exploring the uncharted portions of my district. Bugufi and most of the country west of Lake Victoria had not been mapped in any detail. This was true especially of the river systems. I knew of no map that gave any information on the source of the Ruvuvu, which was assumed to rise somewhere in Burundi, no one knew exactly where. To reach its source would mean struggling for miles through almost impenetrable bush. I was more interested in its downward, northerly course, which I was determined one day to explore. On the north-west side of Bugufi, another river flowed from the interior of Ruanda; this, according to the vague map I already possessed, could be the Kagera; but I had no idea of its course, except that it flowed eastwards to Lake Victoria. Nor had I any idea of its size, nor of its connection, if any, with other rivers. As far as I knew, it touched no part of the Bugufi territory that I had so far visited. The Ruvuvu flowed to the north-east, also towards the lake, but how far could only be guessed. The only way of determining its course was to travel down it in a dug-out canoe; ordinary bark canoes would not have stood up to attacks by hippopotami, which abounded in the Ruvuvu.

With Mapera and four Barundi boatmen, skilled paddlers, I set out downstream early one morning. Our canoe had been hollowed out of a particularly tough tree, and was extremely heavy. For about four miles from our embarkation point there was habitation along the west bank and no sign of hippo. Then we entered a stretch of water, several miles long, with high reeds on each side extending well out into the river. Here we heard the hippos grunting and splashing in the reeds, and at times they would surface to have a look at us. They did not venture nearer than twenty or thirty yards, but that was quite enough for our liking. I had nothing more powerful than a double-barrelled shot-gun. I should, of course, have carried a rifle, but it was now too late to think of that.

About 5 p.m. we entered a stretch of water with habitation on the west bank and a welcome absence of reeds, and a broad expanse of open country with huts and cultivation and some cattle in view. We were free for the time being from the threats of hippo. Close on 6 p.m. as the light began to fade, we anchored our canoe and pitched camp for the night. We had paddled since early morning and covered, with the aid of the current, thirty or forty miles. So far our course had been through a broad and deep river; we had not passed rapids or shallow water. We had no idea where this voyage would lead us, but we hoped that from now on the river we were exploring would continue to flow through open country.

Next day at dawn we went on, and soon entered another stretch with thick reeds obscuring either bank and obviously sheltering hippo. We travelled unmolested, although hippo continued surfacing to inspect us. Our principal danger was that this might be the season when the cows were rearing their young in the reeds; if so, the males would resent the approach of strangers.

Shortly after two o'clock we hear a loud roar perhaps a quarter of a mile away, resembling the noise of a waterfall or cataract. I told the canoemen to bring us to the east bank and hug the reeds for the rest of the way. We had hardly reached the reeds when the end of the canoe where I was seated heaved out of the water. Just beneath me and close enough to touch was the grey back of an outsize male hippo. The canoe did not capsize, being too heavy; but we grabbed the tall reeds and held on grimly. Then our attacker submerged and the canoe slid back upright into the water. We waited anxiously for the next attack, but after a few seconds the hippo surfaced less than ten yards from us. Meanwhile I had loaded the shot-gun, and now I fired. The animal dived, the water around us churned and billowed like a tidal wave, rocking our canoe violently but not upsetting it. We waited tensely but it next surfaced at least sixty yards away puffing and grunting with rage. As it was clear that we could go no further by water, we pulled our canoe through the reeds to the bank, on tenterhooks in case we aroused more hippos. Here we were confronted by the densest belt of thorn bush imaginable, which canoemen could fortunately cut through with their pangas. We came out on to an escarpment, from which we looked down to a deep gorge, into which poured a magnificent waterfall from a height of over a hundred feet. The noise was deafening and a huge cloud of spray almost obscured the broad pool into which the river fell. This cataract, although it did not compare in size with the Victoria Falls on the Zambezi, was still large enough to be classed among nature's great showpieces.

From our vantage point we could look back upstream. About a hundred yards above the falls another river joined the Ruvuvu; this had to be the Kagera, coming in from Belgian Ruanda. We were now looking down, as I believed, on the final form of the Kagera as it made its way to Lake Victoria. Across the river was Ruanda, and far to the north-east we could see into Uganda. Had

The Rusumo Cataract, just below the confluence of the Ruvuvu and Kagera rivers. Top left is the entrance of the Ruvuvu, and top right the entrance of the Kagera.

we not been attacked by the hippo we might have reached the confluence of the two rivers in our canoe and in so doing, come dangerously near the falls. Our craft might not have withstood the combined current of two rivers.

I suggested to Mapera that this could be the true source of the Nile. The combined waters of the Ruvuvu and Kagera produced a river of great depth and width flowing on to Victoria. Unless there were other feeder rivers to the lake — and none had yet been discovered — the Kagera had to be accepted as the main source of the Lake's water; if this theory were correct the source of the White Nile consisted of the two rivers and their tributaries that flowed east and north of Bugufi.

Our theory was supported in a strange way. On the shelf where we stood was a tree with a thick but hollow trunk. In Africa such cavities are often the resting places of snakes or other vermin, but out of curiosity I put a stick into the hole and struck a hard object. It was a glass jar with a cork stopper, inside which was a folded piece of paper. The writing was in ink, faded but legible, and in German. The paper was signed and dated 1890 — thirty-eight years before. The message was that here on the date mentioned the Signatory (whose name I do not remember) had discovered the source of the Nile.

I returned the jar and its contents to the tree, and in the fading light we retraced our steps to the canoe, which was still safely moored where we left it. We crossed the Ruvuvu to the west bank, again having to pole our way through high reeds to reach dry land, I with my gun at the ready. There we camped for the night. Two days later, by fast marching, we were back at Ngara and my wattle-and-daub hut.

I did not report my adventures to the Government, as this might have invited the rebuke that exploring African rivers was not part of my administrative duties to the Barundi tribe.

6

LINDI AND TUNDURU

My stay in Bugufi had not earned me any laurels, because on my return from home leave in 1930 I was posted as Assistant District Officer to Lindi, a coastal town in southern Tanganyika with a hinterland of about sixty miles. I was clearly not being given another District for the time being. As I had not yet reached the substantive rank of District Officer, I could not really complain. My District Commissioner was the Hon. Francis Bampfylde.

I had not been more than three months at Lindi when reports came in that famine had broken out at Tunduru, a district 120 miles to the west. Travellers passing through the area had advised the Provincial Commissioner at Lindi of acute food shortages among the tribal populations. The local D.C. had strenuously rebutted these reports, but the P.C. was not satisfied and wanted an independent opinion. Because I now had a reputation as an expert on famines, I was ordered to Tunduru to report. My position was embarrassing: I had to go into the District of another officer, superior in rank to myself, to investigate whether his estimate of the situation in his own District was or was not correct.

It was the dry season and I made the journey comfortably by car over a reasonably good road, which ran through Masasi and Tunduru to our most westerly district of Songea, and thence to Mbamba Bay on the lake.

At Tunduru, as I expected, the District Commissioner, whom I shall call D., gave me a chilly reception. He scoffed at the idea of famine and insisted that the Africans were fooling us. To arrive at my own view I immediately set out on a three weeks' village-to-village tour of the district on foot, questioning everybody I met and inspecting as wide an area as possible. I also looked closely at every woman and child I could find. As day followed day in my tramping of the countryside I grew convinced D. was completely misreading the situation, and that there was an acute food shortage. It was the familiar pattern of a tribe living at a bare subsistence level and being caught without reserves when the seasonal rains failed. I officially reported that famine existed and that a relief campaign should be mounted.

Living at that time at Tunduru was an ex-Rhodesian policeman, Gerald Sibold, who ran a transport business between Lindi and

Songea in partnership with an ex-army officer named Carnegie Browne, who looked after the Lindi end of the business. Sibold was in close touch with the Tunduru tribes and confirmed my report. He told me that he had frequently warned D. about this famine, but that D. had ignored his advice, suggesting that a declaration of famine would bring commercial benefit to Sibold's transport company. Meanwhile I remained at Tunduru, camped near the D.C.'s headquarters, awaiting instructions from the P.C. at Lindi. These, when they came, were sent direct to D., who was informed that my report on the famine had been accepted and that he could retain my services to assist with the administration of relief. D. reasserted his stubborn rejection of the idea of famine, and requested me to arrange my return to Lindi without delay. My position was now highly embarrassing; D. was defying Provincial instructions and was trying to involve me in his defiance. I could do only one thing, which was to send a private report and request for further instructions to the Provincial Commissioner. Meanwhile time was passing. If we waited much longer we would not be able to get supplies through by motor transport before the rains came. Without delay a reply came from the P.C. instructing D. to hand over the administration of Tunduru to me and report to Lindi. Thus I was installed as Acting District Commissioner with the special duty of controlling a famine. A visit to Tunduru that had originally been planned to last three weeks would now be extended to nine months.

Sibold told me a strange story about D. He was in the habit of going for a long walk every evening, wearing a hat. When, towards sunset, he came to the point of turning for home he would hang his hat on a convenient tree and proceed on his way back hatless. The first African who passed that way after him and saw the hat was expected to bring it to D.'s house and hand it to his servants, even if he was going in the opposite direction with a long journey ahead of him. If he ignored the hat, he would be haunted by the fear that D.'s intelligence system would catch up with him. I did not believe this story until I myself went for a walk one evening while D. was still in charge, and saw the hat hanging on a tree.

I learned from another source of a different side to D.'s character His predecessor had been a young officer, P. When D. was taking over the district he noticed that P. had a pair of elephant tusks in his loads; he inspected the ivory register but could find no reference to these tusks which, he discovered, came from a rogue bull elephant shot by one of the game scouts. They had been taken to the District Office but not registered, though they had been given the Government stamp to make them saleable. P. confessed his guilt, and was allowed to return the tusks to store, where they were duly registered and included in Government stock. If D. had reported this serious breach of duty, P. would almost certainly have been dismissed, but he survived to become a Provincial Commissioner many years later.

Happily we were prepared in time for the emergency at Tunduru, not as in Bugufi where the famine was already raging before we could get to grips with it. Also we could use motor transport instead of waiting weary weeks while bearers struggled through the bush with loads on their heads. Thanks to the substantial help give us by Sibold's transport organisation, we obtained all the supplies we needed before the roads were closed. Furthermore, Sibold's lorries were able to carry the food to the different distribution centres I had organised.

I carried out the same relief routine as at Bugufi, dividing the district into areas, each one with its own food store to which supplies were allocated in proportion to its population. It took us five months to overcome the famine, but we were spared the heavy death toll there had been in Bugufi. We were fortunate too in obtaining plenty of maize, the people's staple diet, which we were able to supplement with other foods, such as beans, with a good protein content. Milk, however, was very scarce for this was another of those tsetse belts where cattle could not live. It was fortunate that African mothers in this district breast-fed their children up to the age of two years.

After every famine there is the problem of re-establishing seed supplies. Following the Bugufi plan, I created a communal farm of ten acres. Again, the ground was cleared by the men and the maize seed planted by the women. In time a good crop resulted and the seed was distributed through the Native Authority to the village headmen. I never had any means of checking the distribution from headmen to villagers, but I often suspected that the headmen made a good thing out of it. They were certainly in a strong position to do so: although the distribution was officially free, people would gladly pay something for an extra ration of seed.

During my stay in Tunduru reports constantly reached us of man-eating lions haunting villages and snatching unwary victims as they walked the narrow bush paths. The menace was too widespread for normal trapping routines, as in Bugufi. I could only advise the chiefs and headmen to warn their people never to travel singly — or unarmed — in the bush.

While I was busily engaged in combating famine among the Tunduru Africans I myself became the victim of a kind of famine, in the sense that my own stocks of tinned food and whisky, which I had laid in before the rainy season, soon ran out. Sibold and I, being the only Europeans in the district, naturally congregated when time and duty permitted: I enjoyed his society and he enjoyed my whisky. With several months still to go I found myself without any form of alcoholic drink. This was a real hardship. For the rest of my stay in Tunduru I had to make do with juice squeezed from the wild limes of the district. When my tinned rations ran out I was in a really bad way. In Lindi there was no meat but we could always fish from the sea. In Tunduru there was neither fish nor meat; nor did any vegetables grow except for a barely edible wild spinach which grew in the bush. Without the native chickens, which were available, I would have starved. My resourceful African cook prepared a daily diet of chicken, spinach and, in place of potato, a cake made from ground cassava. He also made soup from chicken bones. This was my diet for five months. I had some tea in reserve, but no milk, so with the lime juice I was able to drink a kind of Russian tea.

At last the time came for my return to Lindi — it was at the end of the first twelve months of my tour. Most of the remaining eighteen months were spent in routine administration, which included looking after certain Native Authorities that Bampfylde had assigned to my care.

There was one short break in my routine. District Officers, in their capacity as magistrates, were subject to the supervision and control of the High Court, which had its headquarters at Dar-es-Salaam. All cases, civil or criminal, tried by these officers had, if called for, to be submitted for the inspection of the High Court judges. Even when there had been no appeal, a judge could quash a conviction if on inspecting the record he was satisfied that the case has been badly tried and a conviction wrongly recorded. He could also order a re-trial. If an officer had a succession of cases that displeased the High Court, he could be barred for a stated time from trying further cases.

A District Officer's magisterial jurisdiction was limited to the passing of sentences of imprisonment not exceeding four years; the trial of the more serious crimes such as rape, manslaughter and murder was outside his powers. However, the High Court could, by special order, confer jurisdiction upon him to try one or other of these serious crimes, if it considered him fit. The judges were apparently pleased with my court work, because an order arrived at Lindi one day appointing me to try a murder case at Kilwa. This was an old Arab settlement on the coast about eighty miles to the north. It had been a flourishing port in the old days when the Arab *dhows* plied between Arabia and East Africa carrying spices and carpets one way and large consignments of African slaves the other. Now it was nearly a ghost town with a population of half-caste Arabs and detribalised Africans.

The murder case was to be prosecuted by a Sikh inspector of police from Lindi, so he and I set off together at noon one day in my box-body Ford. We arrived in Kilwa the following morning at 8 a.m., completely exhausted. That we should have spent twenty hours covering eighty miles tells its own story. Long sections of the coast road had deep ruts made by lorries that had travelled along it during the rains. These had become brick-hard from weeks of sunshine. For most of the journey therefore, we drove in low-gear, with the car balancing on the edge of ruts which were too deep for its ground clearance. At times we made diversions into the forest alongside our route; to do this we had to clear the bush at night by the light of the car lamps.

When the case came up for trial I found that the accused, an African, had no one to defend him. This often happened. Although Government was prepared to provide counsel to defend Africans charged with murder, the fees were not sufficient to induce Indian advocates, the only ones available, to make long journeys to isolated places like Kilwa. I had therefore to be both judge and defending counsel which meant cross-examining every prosecution witness on the prisoner's behalf. In trials of this nature the presiding judge acts without a jury, but is provided with the services of three African assessors, preferably of the same tribe as the accused, whose principal function is to interpret any tribal custom that may have a bearing on the case. They are also invited to give their opinion as to the accused's guilt or innocence, but the judge is not bound by it.

When all the evidence had been heard and the prosecutor had summed up for the Crown I asked the assessors for their opinions: Their unanimous opinion was: 'The prisoner is not guilty because there was no woman involved in the case.' This had no bearing on the evidence and was a kind of inverted rendering of the famous dictum 'cherchez la femme', but it was the kind of irrelevant opinion to be expected from African assessors. However, I had arrived at a similar conclusion, if for different reasons, and acquitted the accused. I am happy to say that the High Court in due course approved my verdict.

Our journey back to Lindi was a repetition of our previous adventures, except that this time we knew what to expect and were better prepared.

Twelve months after my return from Tunduru, Bampfylde went on leave and was succeeded by S. V. Cooke, an officer transferred from Kenya Colony. Cooke had become involved in a controversy with the European Planters' Association there over a question of African land rights. One needed courage to argue with that powerful organisation, whether one was in the right or in the wrong. It proved too strong for Cooke, and he had to be moved to another sphere of activity—which happened to be Lindi. I enjoyed working with him until I went on leave six months later, having completed my full stint of thirty months.

In the Colonial Service of my day the minimum tour an officer was required to serve was twenty months and the maximum thirty months. If an officer wanted six months' leave at home he had to complete the maximum. If he wished to serve more than thirty months so as to earn additional leave, he was obliged to undergo a medical examination.

People often wondered why the maximum tour was fixed at thirty months. A knowledgeable colleague volunteered the explanation that thirty months was the time it took Burton and Speke to travel from the coast to Lake Tanganyika and back, during their journey in search of the source of the Nile.

7

KOROGWE

I returned to Tanga from home leave in August 1933, having been called to the English Bar at Gray's Inn. I had already taken an LL.B degree at Trinity College, Dublin, before entering the colonial service, but when I realised how much of a District Officer's time was taken up with court and other legal work, I decided to pursue my law studies to the point of qualifying as a barrister.

All administrative officers were *ex-officio* magistrates, whether they knew any law or not. Confirmation of appointment as an Assistant District Officer after the two years' probationary period depended, among other things, on the candidate's passing an examination on the legal codes applicable to the territory, but no other test of an officer's capacity for hearing court cases was required. Although all cases tried by administrative officers had to pass the scrutiny of the local High Court, judges had to be selective in calling for cases from the lower courts, otherwise they would have been deluged by revisionary work. From comments I had seen on other officers' case records, I was only too well aware of the general dissatisfaction the judges felt for the work of 'amateur magistrates' as they called us, and I admit that some of their criticisms were justified. The judges would have liked all subordinate court work done by professional magistrates, but this, financially, was a pipe-dream. The budget of a territory with a sparse and scattered African population paying a low rate of tax could not support a specially paid class of magistrates; hence the professionals were limited to one or two large towns like Tanga and Dar-es-Salaam. Over the rest of the country the subordinate courts had to be operated by the administration.

It was a case of running the country on the cheap, with the District Commissioners and their British staffs as dogsbodies. But there was no other way if the burden were not to be thrown on the British taxpayer at home. In my twenty-two years of service I must have tried nearly 2,000 cases, the great majority criminal. Also, under the extended jurisdiction powers already mentioned, I tried at least six capital cases and a dozen others outside the jurisdiction of the ordinary first-class magistrate, such as rapes and man-slaughters.

The system created friction between the Administration and the High Court, because administrative officers resented the occasional strictures of High Court judges, and it must be confessed that certain officers grew restive under the restrictions imposed on them by such tiresome rules as the laws of evidence. If they did not feel contempt for the law, they felt contempt for the experts who expounded it for their instruction and benefit. It thus happened that any officer who heeded the lessons from the judges and endeavoured to improve his efficiency as a magistrate by studying for the Bar exposed himself to the suspicion that he was siding with the High Court against his own set.

Thus I found that my efforts to improve my capacity as an administrator by being called to the Bar were a hindrance rather than a help to my administrative career. From time to time I was switched from my administrative duties to fill some legal gap while the substantive holder of the post was on leave or otherwise occupied. This not only affected my career prospects but my enjoyment of the work. I had come to Africa to take part in district administration, not to sit in an office at headquarters writing legal minutes or investigating somebody's bankruptcy. I felt resentment at these secondments from my normal duties which I took no pains to conceal.

The first of these secondments happened when I arrived in Tanga. The Provincial Commissioner greeted me with the news that he had hoped to give me the choice of one out of three districts, but that meanwhile a temporary vacancy existed in the Public Trustee's Department which I was required to fill until a new appointment arrived from home. I was therefore obliged to act as a stop-gap Public Trustee until January 1934, when I was released to return to the Administration. Meanwhile all three Districts had been filled, and I was posted as Assistant District Officer to Korogwe under a District Commissioner, C., who was only a few weeks senior to myself in the service. However C. was due to leave the District in a few weeks, and I was then to take over. At the time I had no real ground of complaint, because I was substantively an A.D.O. and my promotion to the rank of District Officer was not due for another few months.

I could not stay idle while waiting to take over from C. As he was all for a quiet life and did not care much for safari and tent life, he left to me the outside running of the District while he looked after the office work. Great Britain and the world were then in the throes of a great slump, which had spread like an epidemic over Africa, bringing the revenues of the Territory to a low ebb. All colonial officers were suffering a 10 per cent cut in their salaries, and their camp allowance of 8 shillings a night for safari had been withdrawn. Officers now had to travel on tours of inspection at their own expense. Their salary cuts and allowances were not restored for another three years, and the original deductions from their salaries were never refunded. Sisal, the main agricultural export of Tanganyika, had fallen heavily in price and the brunt of this was borne by the African labourers on the sisal estates. These people now had the greatest difficulty in paying their taxes, and to crown everything one of the severest plagues of locusts within living memory devastated African foodcrops, especially in the valleys and lowlands, where the softer soils were admirably suited to the laying and hatching of locusts' eggs. Korogwe District was one of the main sufferers. One day in my car I drove into a locust swarm so thick that I could see nothing ahead of me and was brought to a stop. I had to wait half an hour until it passed. I wondered if I was about to encounter my third famine.

The District was not unknown to me. As a young A.D.O. towards the end of my first tour I had opened the first administrative offices here when it had been a sub-District of Lushoto. It was now a District in its own right, but as the main tribe (the Wasambaa) occupied all the Usambara country, of which Lushoto and Korogwe were geographically and ethnically parts, one Native Authority ruled over the Africans in both Districts. Korogwe District ran northwards at the foot of the western range of the Usambara mountains through Mashewa and the Luengera valley to the Bombo river valley and the sub-chiefdom of Daluni. It may be briefly described as including all the valley lands east, south and west of the Usambara range as well as the small eastern Usambara sub-range which contained Amani. It also included a small range of hills immediately overlooking Korogwe in which was the former German health centre of Vugiri, all the buildings of which were excellently preserved, and two tea estates owned by British planters. The District Offices and staff quarters were in the damp and hot lowlands, which were full of mosquitoes and other pests. I always wondered why the District could not have been administered from the much healthier atmosphere of Vugiri. One reason vouchsafed to me for retaining Korogwe as District headquarters was that it was near to the sisal estates and sisal managers would complain if they had to travel to Vugiri every time they had business with the District Commissioner. I suspected that another reason was that governments do not like to house their officers in places that are too healthy lest this should discourage travelling on safari in less attractive areas. I used Vugiri, when I could, mainly as a week-end retreat from the heat of the plains.

The sisal estates were concentrated around Korogwe itself and in the north-western section that ran along the lowlands from Korogwe to Makuyuni. Sisal likes hot low-lying country, and the conditions for its production here were ideal. There was also plenty of good land for growing African crops such as maize, cassava and sweet potatoes. It was good cotton country, but no cotton had so far been grown.

I gave my attention first to the Luengera valley and made my first trip there in February 1934. This valley, sixty miles long, was one of the most fertile parts of Tanganyika Territory, with rich soil well watered by the Luengera and Bombo rivers. Yet I found there an extensive food shortage and a discouraging tax position. Both of these conditions were tied up with the slump in sisal and the low wages on the estates, where a high proportion of the male population worked. Matters had been made worse by the locust plague. All the maize grown in the valley had been destroyed and the people existed on the few potato crops they had planted.

I held a meeting at every sub-chief's headquarters and found that over 60 per cent of our adult taxpayers, of whom there were about 20,000, were in default, some for two years or longer. The local Hut and Poll Tax was ten shillings, but when a year previously the trade depression had begun to bite hard, the Government had devised a system of tax payments by instalments. An African would be given a card with ten spaces on it, each representing one shilling; he could buy a one shilling stamp or more at a time and when the card was full hand it in to his Native Authority and receive a full tax-receipt in exchange. The system was only partly successful, as it depended on the co-operation of estate managers, which they did not always give. Sisal managers were averse to disturbing their workers by making them stamp their cards at regular intervals, and where a manager did try to co-operate, his workers often deserted to other estates where the stamping of cards was not too rigorously applied. Indeed some estates deliberately encouraged desertion of labour from their neighbours by letting it be known that the deserters would not be worried about purchasing tax stamps. Furthermore other Africans who had not paid or did not wish to pay their tax instalments used the sisal estates as havens of refuge against their tax-collecting Native Authorities. If this were allowed to continue, the Native Authority and its treasury would become bankrupt and the Central Government would run seriously short of funds. C. had not improved the position by exempting the people in the sub-chiefdom of Mashewa from payment of their two years' arrears of tax on the grounds of bad harvests—an unwise policy which encouraged laziness. I decided to hold my hand until I took over the district.

The crop situation and the general laxity of the Native Authorities involved me in some unpleasant incidents. I held a meeting at Mashewa, which revealed that of the 400 adult males who attended, most of them against their will, less than ten had paid tax during the past two years. The sub-chief's registers also showed that nearly 1,000 registered taxpayers had long been in default.

Among the 400 at the meeting was one particularly ill-dressed man wearing a very dirty cap. He, like most of those present, had surly manners. I told him to remove his cap when I addressed him, but he ignored my request, so I boxed his ears. I was only then informed that he was the African priest of the local Lutheran mission. My embarrassment was relieved when I found that he was also a tax defaulter, and I admonished him for the bad example he was setting the others. However, I apologised to him and later visited his mission. We became good friends, and he did his best to co-operate with my campaigns for harder work and more crops.

The second incident was to have far-reaching results. It occurred in Daluni at the top of the valley a stronghold of the Universities Mission to Central Africa, many of its inhabitants being baptised members of the Anglican Church. The head of the mission was the Bishop of Zanzibar, whose headquarters were at Muhesa, twenty miles south-west of Tanga; his diocese covered the eastern belt of Tanganyika as well as the island of Zanzibar. My activities, aimed at improving the food supplies and staving off all danger of shortage, brought me into conflict with his powerful and influential organisation.

The entire Luengera district was short of food and the tax position was calamitous. When I walked into the principal village of Daluni, within sight of the mission station, the scene that met my eyes filled me with anger. In the fields the women were toiling away at clearing the ground for planting, while the male population, consisting mostly of young men, took its ease playing an African game somewhat resembling marbles. With the stick that I was carrying I belaboured them one and all, and ordered them to take off their nice clean *kanzus*, take up their hoes and get into the fields alongside their women. The same day I visited other villages and came across similar scenes where the men were lolling about and the women were doing the planting work. I treated all these idlers in the same way, and soon the word went about that a savage *bwana* was raging through the district beating everybody up.

A month later I received a letter from the Provincial Commissioner giving a list of charges brought against me by the U.M.C.A. mission at Daluni. One of my accusers was the sub-chief of Mashewa, whom I had dismissed for idleness and incompetence. I was supposed to have knocked him down and imprisoned him for three days. There were other equally preposterous charges. Every malcontent who had suffered chastisement from me was anxious to get in on the act. These charges had been written down by the English

mission sister at Daluni to the dictation of my accusers; no attempt
had been made to check on their truth.

I was invited to answer the charges in writing. This was given to
the officer holding the inquiry, but I was not allowed to be present
and cross-examine the witnesses; it was explained that Africans
might be afraid of speaking openly in my presence. The outcome
was that most of the complainants ratted when examined in court,
and the mission staff who had involved themselves at the begining
never turned up at the hearing. Nevertheless I had to wait several
weeks for the verdict of the inquiry and the Government's decision
which was that I had 'acted with vigour, discretion and good sense'.

Some months later I returned to my bungalow one evening to
find the Bishop of Masasi and his chaplain waiting for me. I greeted
these gentlemen with courtesy and offered them hospitality. We
chatted about many matters and the Bishop promised the co-
operation of the mission in my campaign to improve food production
and fight the locusts; neither of us referred to the Daluni incident.

As soon as I took over the district from C., I had to tackle the twin
problems of food shortage and locust infestation, both of which were
closely connected with the serious fall in tax revenue. The locusts
remained with us for nearly another year: I often looked up to the
sky and saw it darkened by a swarm, which sometimes extended
as far as the eye could see. Government had issued orders through
the Native Authorities that all able-bodied Africans were to be
mobilised to beat the hoppers, i.e. the young locusts hatched out
from the eggs. I told the chiefs and headmen to ignore these orders
and instead to encourage their people to grow crops that were
immune to locust attack. For this purpose I had an order passed
by the Native Authority making it compulsory for every taxpayer
to grow cassava and sweet potatoes; imprisonment was prescribed
for any one disobeying it. It would be no defence for a taxpayer to
say that he was working on a sisal estate and could not return to
his village. No one was exempted except the old and the sick. In all,
about 200 people went to gaol, most of them sentenced by the
native courts, but we achieved the desired results; by December
1934 over 20,000 acres of these crops had been planted and the
district was saved from the threat of famine. This represented about
one acre per taxpayer. I discouraged the planting of maize while
the locusts were around: locusts delight in maize, but stay away
from cassava and sweet potatoes—and, significantly, from cotton.

In May 1934 I was invited to the port of Tanga, then being
visited by a British cruiser of the East Indies squadron, to play
rugby and cricket against the sailors, and so took a welcome break
of three or four days. At the end of the month Frederick Crawford

came from neighbouring Handeni to be my Assistant District Officer. He was later to become one of our best known colonial administrators and as Sir Frederick Crawford was the last Governor of Uganda before that colony achieved independence. He stayed with me until his home leave fell due in January 1935. During our time together he was a loyal and trusted colleague, and gave me efficient support in the administration of the District. I never again had the good fortune to work with him; he later gravitated to the Governor's secretariat where his qualities were quickly recognised and marked him out for advancement to the higher echelons of administration.

The tax problem was our biggest worry. As I have already mentioned, C. had complicated matters by exempting the 1,000 defaulting taxpayers of Mashewa: I cancelled this exemption without delay. Every adult male throughout the District was told that he must pay all arrears or else meet his obligations by public work, to be determined by myself. There would be plenty of this. Tax labour would not fill the coffers of the treasury, but it would encourage those who had money to pay, while those who were without money could work on improving the roads.

In an African community it was bad economics to raise money by selling food. I was anxious to develop a cash crop. The Agricultural Department advised that the soil of the valleys and the climate were suitable for cotton, but before I finally committed myself to a cotton policy it was essential that I should make sure of a market. It would be disastrous to encourage Africans to grow this crop if there were to be no buyers. Therefore I made contact with a leading firm of Indian cotton merchants in Tanga and obtained from them an assurance that they would buy all the cotton produced at the prevailing market price. Thus armed with the certainty of a market, I decided to push ahead with cotton cultivation. In this campaign I was assisted and advised by an agricultural officer called Thomas, a qualified agronomist who had spent his earlier career in the tea gardens of Java. He was as knowledgeable about cotton as about tea, and was a stimulating campaigner. But it was an arduous campaign because few of our Africans had ever planted cotton before, and they were sceptical of our assurances that locusts would not attack it.

We made our first safaris in April, touring all the sub-chief's headquarters in the Luengera and Makuyuni valleys and distributing cotton seed at each. If our efforts were to succeed it was essential that every sub-chief should give a lead by having his own cotton patch: this was achieved. I made it clear that cotton planting was not compulsory, as with the food crops, but said that any able-

bodied man who refused to make a trial planting would be regarded
as being indifferent to the interests of his community and undeserv-
ing of the same consideration as those who co-operated. At the
same time I compromised on the tax position, saying that of the
two years' tax owed by nearly everyone, the first year could be met
by labour on public projects, while payment of the second year
would be deferred until after the cotton markets. Those who did
not plant would be required to pay all two years at once or alter-
natively to liquidate their debt by labour.

While on this safari I took the opportunity of getting rid of a few
useless chiefs and headmen and appointing others who were proposed to me by the local elders; all these new appointments had
to be confirmed by the Chief of the Wasambaa at Vuga. This policy
brought results, especially in Mashewa, where the new Sub-Chief,
an elderly man named Wali, brought about many welcome changes.

Some administrative officers made the mistake of going through
their Districts issuing orders but not returning soon enough to see
if they had been carried out. Thomas and I returned in May to see
how much cotton had been planted. The result was not encouraging,
as only about a quarter of those who had received seed had planted
it. I therefore decided to make a selective recruitment of tax-
defaulters among the non-planters, and put them on road work.

The road from Korogwe through the Luengera valley was in
poor condition. If the cotton markets were to be supplied in October
this road had to be put in good order. More than 500 tax labourers
from every part of the valley were divided into gangs and put to
work. As men completed their tax labour they were replaced by
other defaulters. All was under competent supervision, and by
October the road, by the local standards, was in good condition.
It was, of course, a dry-weather earth road and when the short
rains came in December it would again deteriorate. It was sufficient that it should hold for the cotton markets.

The recruitment of tax labour had a stimulating effect on cotton
planting, and by the end of June the acreage under cultivation had
greatly increased. In Sub-Chief Wali's region of Mashewa 120
cotton planters, who had already paid all their taxes, turned out
voluntarily and repaired a large section of the road without payment. This was indeed a promising portent.

The first cotton markets opened in mid-October. The Indian
merchants, true to their word, turned up complete with lorries.
I arranged with them where and when the markets were to be held,
so that Thomas and I could personally supervise all purchasing
and advise the sub-chiefs where and when to assemble the sellers.
The first markets were not exciting, but we were not expecting

large results in the opening stages of the campaign. They produced about thirty tons. The second markets in November, which Crawford supervised, produced seventy-five tons. This proved two valuable points—first that if Africans grew cotton they could sell it at a fair market price and, secondly, that the grower could provide tax money from his cotton crop without having to draw on his food supply. The better the grade of cotton the better the price. There was difficulty about this in the beginning, but Thomas took great trouble to give lectures on correct grading, and in time the growers understood the technique.

We had won an important propaganda battle. A few growers, went away from the markets with 100 shillings or more in their pockets, depending upon their industry. With tax at 10 shillings this meant a balance of 90 shillings. A man who worked for two months on his cotton plot could earn ten times the amount of his annual wages on a sisal estate. Paying tax was no longer a burden for him. By degrees this was grasped by everyone. For example, the small area of Magoma brought only one and a half tons to the 1934 markets but 150 tons to the 1936 markets. While this colossal rate of increase could not be matched elsewhere, the overall developments of the original campaign were very impressive. The 100 tons of 1934 became 1,500 tons in 1935 and more than 3,000 tons in 1936. Plans for building a cotton ginnery at Korogwe in 1935 were put in hand, but I had left before they came to fruition.

In January 1935 Thomas went on leave and was succeeded by a new agricultural officer, Swynnerton, who carried on the good work begun by Thomas enthusiastically and competently. But we now ran into new difficulties concerning the sisal estates in the District. My relations with them were mostly routine; under the Labour Ordinance I functioned as an Inspector of Labour and had free access to any estate during working hours to inspect labour conditions, hear complaints from either side, or round up tax defaulters. Unless they were carried out tactfully, these duties might cause friction between the District Commissioner and an estate manager. However, although official policy at times conflicted with the commercial interests of an estate, my personal relations with most of the managers were friendly. We occasionally enjoyed social evenings together, and I often entertained my planter friends for the weekend at Vugiri.

However, the promotion of cotton production brought to a head the major labour problems of the estates. The heavy fall in sisal prices had compelled the estates to reduce wages by as much as 25 per cent — to the point where Africans had trouble not only in finding their tax money but in feeding their families. There was certainly no spare cash to buy cloth for their wives. Then came the cotton markets, when the sisal labourers saw their fellow-tribesmen coming away with many times their tax money in their pockets, all collected in one morning and for a few weeks' work on a cotton patch. They saw that these people had plenty of money for cloth and other luxuries such as European oil lamps and even bicycles. It was not long before an exodus began from the estates to the cotton fields, and in the second planting season there was a universal demand for seed. Because in the pre-cotton days local labour had been plentiful and cheap, few estates had bothered to recruit workers from up-country districts. Now they were suddenly faced with an actute shortage and began to make threatening noises, first to me and later at a higher level. The Tanganyika Planters' Association became involved.

I now had to be wary. Powerful organisations of this kind usually have the ear of government, and it is dangerous for someone as small as a District Commissioner to join battle with them. I was as tactful as possible to my planter friends, but had to point out to them that under our equal system the individual was free to pursue his livelihood in any way he chose within the law, and that local Africans could not be compelled to work on sisal estates if they preferred some other way of earning money. I suggested that the best way to counter the fall-off in labour was either to increase wages or to recruit from outside.

The estates had no intention of adopting either of these remedies. Through their Association they chose another way, which was revealed to me when an order came from the Government directing me not to distribute cotton seed or to encourage planting in areas that adjoined or were close to sisal estates. This meant denying seed to all Africans in the Korogwe-Maurui-Makutuni valley. The order had, of course, to be obeyed in the letter if not in the spirit. I told the sub-chiefs in this valley that I had been forbidden to give any seed to their people, but that I could not prevent their obtaining it from the Native Authorities elsewhere, as long as they were willing to go to the non-restricted parts and collect it for themselves. Judging by later market results this is what they did. Subsequent increases in cotton production proved the ineffectiveness of a policy that lacked popular support. Cotton growing became established in the Korogwe district and nothing short of prohibition or the deliberate closing of markets could stop it.

In the coastal belt of Tanganyika the conflict of interests between the African cultivator and the sisal planter produced an acute dilemma. Sisal was a major item in the Territory's economy, and millions of pounds had been invested in its production. While the price was high the labourer had a reasonable return for his labour, but with the slump on the market he suffered cuts in wages, and his lot was hard if there were no alternative means of earning money.

At the time of which I write sisal production was going through a crisis, and its collapse would have been disastrous for the Territory's finances. The problem was to strike a balance between protection for it and the welfare of the local African: was he to be denied the opportunity of creating wealth for himself on his own plot of ground, simply to provide cheap labour for an industry in which he would not share any of the profits?

The answer in a cotton-growing area was twofold — first, to give the local tribesman full freedom to plant his food and cash crops in their appropriate ration and then to attract him to sisal work in his spare time by generous wages; secondly, to encourage the sisal estates to increase their reliance on contracted labour, of which there was an abundant supply in inland districts. In no other way could we fairly apply the principle of the Mandate that where there was a conflict of interest the rights of the indigenous people were paramount.

Roads are an essential part of any economic programme in a country whose economy is based on agricultural development. They were always one of my administrative interests, and I received an unexpected and unsolicited tribute on account of my Luengara road. An expatriate German who specialised in organising game hunting parties wrote to the Provincial Commissioner expressing his surprise and pleasure at the excellent condition of this road compared with his experience of it in previous years.

After Luengera I turned to the Vugiri road. This was an excellently graded track built by the Germans before the advent of motor-cars. In consequence its corners and bends were too narrow and its surface was roughened by neglect, so that motoring on it could be hazardous. We widened all the corners, built up safety banks and re-surfaced the track. As this road led to two estates beyond Vugiri it was especially important, and the tea planters were grateful for our attention to it.

There was no direct communication between the Agricultural Research Station at Amani, within the district, and the Korogwe District Office. Amani, with its staff of highly qualified scientists who served the whole of British East Africa, had but one outlet, the road to Tanga. Although the distance to Korogwe was only 35 miles on foot, safari travellers by car to the western Usambaras had to travel down the Tanga road to Muhesa and thence along the Tanga-Korogwe road, a detour of nearly 80 miles. When, early in 1934, the Director of the Institute suggested to me the possibility

of a more direct route by way of the Luengera valley, I made
inquiries from the sub-chiefs of Daluni and Amani, and learned
that the Germans had used a pony-track from the valley to the
Amani hills. At the first opportunity I traversed this track, through
the hills which rose 3,000 feet from the valley to Amani itself. It
was a rough journey but the grade was adequate. Equipment
would be needed to blast through the rock formations that were
plentiful on the path; also, many hairpin bends would have to be
constructed. It was a pity there were no elephant tracks. I could
supply tax-default labour and supervision, but had no money for
explosives or expensive tools. When I reached Amani I talked again
with the Director, and he agreed to have a survey carried out by his
engineer; if it was favourable, he would co-operate with materials,
tools and supervision if I supplied the labour. A month later, after a
favourable report from the engineer, we met again and agreed that
work should begin at both ends simultaneously. A gang under the
Director's supervision would start at the top, working downhill,
and a gang under my control would work uphill from the Luengera
valley. I put my gang under a reliable German supervisor whom I
recruited specially; he was a planter who had fallen on bad times,
but he had a good reputation with Africans. I could rely on him to
see that the labourers were properly fed and fairly treated.

Place-names will mean nothing to most readers because they are
not shown even on the large-scale maps of today but, for the sake of
the record, the road was surveyed to run from Amani down the
eastern Usambaras to Ngambo and Magunga and enter the
Luengera-Korogwe road at a place called Kerenge. All blasting
was to be done by the Director's staff, and it was estimated that the
road would take six months to complete. The estimate proved
optimistic. Not only was there more blasting, but on the mountain
itself the cutting of the road track and its hair-pin bends was tougher
than we expected. Extensive lengths of forest had to be cleared. In
some places a tree had to be felled every yard. This put a strain on
the supervisors, because their Africans were indifferent to danger
from falling trees.

The work began in April 1934 and the distance to be covered was
fifteen miles. By August nearly nine miles had been completed.
We were behind schedule, and the money was running out. There
were adequate supplies of labour, but not enough cash to feed them
or to pay the supervisor at my end. However, directors of agricultural institutes have influence, and ours was able to squeeze some
extra finance out of the Tanganyika Treasury. $13\frac{1}{2}$ miles had
been completed by the end of January 1935 and a gap of only one
and a half miles remained.

Amani itself stood 3,000 feet up in the eastern Usambaras. With its rich green forested hills with brooks rushing down them it must be one of the most beautiful places in Africa. The climate is temperate at all times and free from the pests and oppressive heat that make life on the plains often so intolerable. Here scientists from England and other parts of the Empire carried on their researches into tropical plant life in up-to-date laboratories for the benefit of many countries. The Institute was a well-organised German foundation, which the British, to their credit, carried on. I could never imagine more delightful surroundings in which to do scientific work, and I always envied the good fortune of the Amani staff.

Cotton, foodcrops and roads were not our only economic interests in Korogwe. There were cattle in small numbers, and African stock owners carried on a trade in hides with Indian dealers. The hides, however, were of poor quality and the prices low until Peter Tully, a veterinary inspector of rare enthusiasm, was posted to the district. Tully spared no effort in helping his African friends to obtain better prices by improving the quality of the hides. He set up special drying sheds in the cattle areas and trained the cattle owners in the scientific methods of flaring and curing. I supported him by ordering that all hides were to be delivered to the curing sheds before being offered for sale. In this I received full co-operation from the Native Authorities, for many of the sub-chiefs and headmen were cattle-owners. Tully never wearied of making tours of inspection and giving demonstrations. The people responded to his teaching, and in time the quality of Korogwe hides reached such a standard that we were able to organise a system of co-operative marketing and sell the entire output of the district to a leather factory in Leeds which gave us a special premium on our products. This involved keeping books to record transactions in detail so that every hide-owner received his allotted share, but Tully regarded this as a labour of love.

For most of 1934, throughout the cotton market period and into the early weeks of 1935, the locusts were with us. Millions of hoppers were also hatching out, to mature into swarms. Nevertheless I stuck to my policy of increasing our acreages of root crops free from attack rather than wasting the people's energies on hopper beating. I had proved my point that our population could survive on a diet of cassava and sweet potatoes and earn a satisfactory income from their cotton plots. There was no harm in their being without maize for a time, and they would surely be able to grow it again.

Then one day at the end of January as I was sitting in my office, the Sub-Chief of Daluni was announced. After the customary greetings I asked him why he had come so far to see me. He said: 'Bwana, can you take out your car and come for a ride with me.' I did as he asked, and ten miles out we came to the first belt of forest. I noticed that the foliage on the trees was unusually thick for the time of the year and of a strangely reddish colour. I mentioned this to my passenger and he said: 'What you see are locusts, and they are dead.' We drove fifty more miles until we came to Daluni. On both sides of the road the trees and the ground were thick with dead locusts. I could only think that multiplicity of numbers and lack of food had killed them, and that perhaps they had been attacked by some fungoid disease or epidemic to which they were vulnerable. If we had spent our time and energy beating hoppers we might have thinned out and thereby strengthened the surviving swarms. When I asked the sub-chief why the locusts had died he replied '*Amri ya mungu*' — 'it is the will of God'.

For weeks in every village throughout the district piles of dead locusts awaited the cooking pot. The Wasambaas enjoyed a full diet of the enemy that had plagued them for so long.

Before closing this chapter I must refer to our work on the township roads. The main road from Tanga to Mombo and Lushoto ran through Korogwe. This was a busy town with a large collection of Indian shops and an African market handling a wide variety of goods. However, its roads became seas of mud during the wet season. Keeping them usable was the responsibility of the District Office, but unless they could be metalled no amount of repair work could be lasting. With every fall of rain the traffic churned up the surface, and motoring became a nightmare. Yet traffic had to be kept moving. We had no supplies of road metal or aggregate, nor had we the machines to roll the metal into the surface even if it had been available. We solved our problem through the help of the Superintendent of Railways, like me a native of Dublin. He had spare supplies of the aggregate that is used as a foundation for railway sleepers. This he railed to me in wagons to Korogwe station.

As a substitute for the roller technique I had two trenches dug lengthwise in the road corresponding to the wheel-track of a large lorry, each trench four feet wide and two feet deep. These were dug for the entire length of the road from the station through the township and a quarter of a mile beyond. Each trench was tightly packed with aggregate and surfaced with ordinary earth. We made rollers out of empty cement barrels, filled with soil, to compact the surface covering and make it smooth. Extra wagons of aggregate had to be railed to us to complete the job, but in the end we produced a mud-free highway. The aggregate packed in the trenches fulfilled the double function of giving firm going to vehicle wheels and draining the rain water. The idea was not original, being already standard practice in Rhodesia.

Early in April 1935, as I was camped in the village of Kerenge, news reached me that I was to take over the district of Mbulu in the Northern Province, 500 miles away, for two months and then return to Korogwe. The District Commissioner there had suffered a nervous breakdown and had to be moved. I was to hold the fort until his successor arrived from leave. I was at this moment helping Swynnerton with the distribution of cotton seed for the 1935 harvest, and resolved to complete the safari before returning to headquarters; I wanted to see the new season started well. What I had already seen was encouraging: everywhere we went, large areas had been cleared for planting, and there was a genuine demand for seed from large numbers of people. Given good rains, we could look forward to a large increase on the previous year's 100 tons. There was now a new atmosphere in the district. At the beginning of my stewardship Africans avoided me and had to be compelled to attend my meetings. Now they came in large numbers with smiling faces, eager to participate in the planting programmes. Crops were plentiful, markets were assured, tax paying was no longer a problem and the locusts had vanished. I could safely leave the new year's agricultural campaign to the capable and energetic Swynnerton and the development of the hide market to Tully. On 13 April I left by train for Moshi en route for Mbulu, supposedly for a two months' stay. I was not to return to Korogwe.

8

MBULU: THE FIRST PHASE

The district of Mbulu was in the Northern Province. I reached
Arusha, the headquarters of the Province, by train from Moshi
on the evening of 14 April 1935 and stayed for two days as the guest
of the Provincial Commissioner and his wife.

Arusha was much sought after by our administrative personnel
because of its cool climate and pleasant surroundings, 4,000 feet
above sea level. On the geologically significant Great Rift Wall,
140 miles to the west, lay the headquarters of the Mbulu district.
The Provincial Commissioner confirmed that I would only be there
for two months and asked me to keep things running until the new
district commissioner arrived from leave.

A motor road of sorts ran from Arusha to Mbulu, along which I
set off by car on the morning of the 16th. I had with me a convoy
containing two British surveyors with cars and lorries. There had been
rain the day before, and the lorries frequently stuck in the mud; it
was 6 o'clock in the evening before we reached the foot of the Rift
Wall at a place ominously named *Mto was Imbu* (the river of the
mosquito). We only rested there for an hour, and then continued
our journey. The road now climbed out of the Arusha plain and by
8.30 p.m. we had covered another 18 miles, by far the best going of
the day. Mbulu, however, was still 50 miles away, and night had
long since fallen. Nevertheless we decided to have a meal and then
push on rather than go to the trouble of pitching tents. This only
brought us greater trouble, because after going only three miles we
encountered a washaway which we only negotiated after hours of
toil in torrential rain. It was now midnight, and we decided to
snatch some sleep. I slept in my car and the two surveyors in the
lee of theirs, with a groundsheet for covering. Starting off next day
at 7 a.m. we covered only 7 miles before noon — so much for the
state of the road. The lorries were the principal cause of delay. I
then decided I had had enough and went on ahead, leaving my
companions to sort out their own problems. The road was now on
higher ground and drier — and the rain had stopped. The scenery
was magnificent — long rolling hills stretching into the distance —
but I was too concerned with the roughness of the track to appreciate
it. Three miles from Mbulu I broke a spring. By reinforcing it with
a block of wood I struggled into the District Headquarters by 5 p.m.

75

I was met at the District Office by Gordon Russell, the Assistant District Officer, and entertained to tea by him and his wife. I never understood why Russell could not have been left in charge until the new man arrived and why I had to come all this way for only two months. However, now that I was there, I resolved to travel as much of the District as possible. From every point of view Mbulu was the most fascinating of all the districts of Tanganyika Territory. From Karatu at the beginning of the Rift Wall through Mbulu itself and into the Barabaig country it was one long chain of broad-capped mountain ranges, interspersed with vast stretches of undulating downs. In the Barabaig country between Katesh and Dongobesh were richly grassed moorlands from which rose the great mountain of Hanang to a height of 14,000 feet. Turning north to Oldeani and beyond you came to the Ngorongoro crater, an extinct volcano sheltering a tremendous variety of game from elephant and rhinoceros to buffalo, giraffe and antelope. It was also the home of the carnivora—lion, leopard, jackal, hyena — and flocks of vultures always hovered there in search of carcasses overlooked by hunters or only partly eaten by their animal killers. South of Oldeani, and running west of Lake Manyara, was a long stretch of moorland bordered by hills from which flowed streams whose waters fed the nearby coffee estates of European settlers. All this country was between 4,000 and 5,000 feet above sea level. Its daytime temperatures were mild and its nights cold. In every European residence I visited, fires at night were the general rule. The same was true of the administrative quarters at Mbulu. At times it was bitterly cold at noon, and I sometimes wore a sweater under my coat to keep warm. Charcoal was the white man's fuel and could be obtained from local charcoal burners. The Africans burned dried cow dung, of which there was an abundance. The black people in these parts must have been naturally resistant to the low temperatures; I have watched a small boy of eight or ten years shepherding the family cattle in a bitter wind and with only a cloth around his loins, his torso completely bare. A white man could never have endured such conditions.

Only a small section of the District differed climatically and scenically from what I have just described. This was a small area at the foot of the Rift Wall, lying between Madukani and Babati. It was inhabited by the Wambugwe, a tribe of only 3,000 people, who were too small in numbers to merit their own administration, and had been placed under the rule of the Gorowa tribe who lived in the high country south from Babati. The Wambugwe country was hot and low-lying, and well stocked with mosquitos. The black soil was suitable for cotton growing.

There was a sprinkling of Europeans in various parts of this attractive land. In the hills near Oldeani lived a tight community of German coffee growers, who had come from Germany as soon as the ban on German immigration, imposed after the 1914-18 war, had been lifted. Many of them came in the guise of hunters, and used their game licences as a cover for their presence in the country. Quietly they squatted in these hills, living in tents and making the minimum of stir. Being off the beaten track they escaped the notice of our administration in those early days until they had planted coffee trees and built themselves temporary shelters. As the local tribe was not using this land, a generous administration allowed them to stay and gave them leasehold titles, which unfortunately contained no clause to forbid sub-letting; hence in the course of time the lessees divided their land into two or three portions to make room for more of their compatriots. Thus the original squatters were multiplied two- and threefold, and by the time I came to Mbulu they were well established. These coffee estates required water, and the sources which their owners proposed to tap were being used by the tribal cattle lower down in the plains.

Close to the Wambugwe country a mixed group of Germans, Greeks, Swedes and other European nationals were growing cotton and tobacco, and even some coffee. It was the first and only time that I had seen coffee and cotton growing close together, because normally these crops require almost opposite climatic conditions. It appeared that there were two different climates here: first a dry spell favouring cotton, and later in the year a wet spell favouring coffee. In fact both crops were grown by means of irrigation furrows that took the water from the Mbulu hills. Tribesmen from the malaria-free highlands used to come down in the daytime and work on the European farms; but they always returned home before nightfall when the mosquitos became busy.

The country west of Babati was the haunt of millionaires and aristocrats from almost every country in Europe. It also attracted one or two rich Americans. Seven miles from Babati an American businessman named Cooper had a coffee estate, and on it a landing strip for his private airplane. Nearby at Dabil a member of the Vanderbilt family was building himself a shooting lodge of cedar, no doubt taken from the summit of Hanang. Two miles from Babati a Scottish earl lived on his coffee estate. His hobby was frequenting cattle markets, where I met him more than once. Close to his estate a Swedish baron also grew coffee, and ten miles away two Russians grew cotton and tobacco. It might be said that these people occupied land which should have been reserved for the indigenous peoples of the District. It is certainly difficult to blame them, given their resources, for settling in these truly magnificent surroundings, away from all the noise and turmoil of Europe!

At Babati itself was a small hotel, the Fig Tree Inn, where most of these people used to meet socially. Its patrons preferred to pay their drink bills by chits — which, as the unfortunate proprietor learned to his cost, were not legal tender.

In the Mbulu District lived four tribes, only one of which, the Wambugwe, was of Bantu stock. I was told on good authority that this tribe followed a custom called *kalema*. A brother or other family relative coming on a visit would be given his host's wife for the night; even an ordinary friend could enjoy this privilege. This alone would explain their lack of population growth; it also indicated the low standing of women in the tribe. The women did all the menial chores. However, I was surprised to learn that they did no work on the family land. This was most unusual, but the explanation was that a wife had no marital security and could be expelled at any time. A husband could divorce her simply by saying 'Go!' Many women, however, had their own independent plots of ground which they cultivated themselves and which no one else could touch. Some months after my first visit to the Wambugwe I reported the existence of *kalema* and suggested that orders should be made forbidding it. I was told not to interfere, but to leave it to the Wambugwe to reform themselves.

The other three tribes inhabited the upper ground of the Rift Wall: the Irakh, the Gorowa (already mentioned) and the Barabaig. These are not Bantu names, and ethnically the tribes were far removed from Bantu origins. The Irakh and Gorowa were closely related. Between them they occupied the northern regions of Mbulu, with Ngorongoro to the north, Lake Eyasi to the west and Lake Manyara and its surrounding country to the east; the southern boundary of this region marched with the northern boundary of the Barabaig country.

Michael, the Chief of the Irakh, had embraced Christianity and was a man of considerable intelligence and energy. If every Native Authority in the Territory had been equally gifted the story of Indirect Rule would have been very different. Michael and Dodo, Chief of the Gorowa, used to meet at regular monthly conferences to discuss the common problems of their tribes.

The name Irakh suggests an Arabic origin, and the language spoken by both Irakh and Gorowa was guttural like Arabic. The Irakh men and women were handsome and well-built, and their sharp features in no way resembled the features of the Bantu negro. The women had soft and delicate complexions, possibly due to their putting only cow's cream, of which there was an abundance, on their faces. There was a strongly rooted superstition that if they washed their faces with water they would become striped like zebras, although water was safe to use on the rest of their bodies. They bathed liberally and were noted for their cleanliness. Cotton cloth was the popular dress, but the young unmarried girls wore only a skirt leaving their bodies bare from the waist upwards. It was only after marriage that they covered their breasts. I have found this custom in other tribes, and one explanation is that the bachelors of the tribe required to know how the women whom they fancied looked without clothes before they committed themselves to matrimony. Pre-marital chastity was imposed by custom, but breach of it was not drastically punished as in some other tribes. The erring male was required to pay in compensation the value of the girl's dowry if she had been married as a virgin. There was sense in this rule, because the man's family would put pressure on him to marry the girl rather than have the dowry money thrown away. Liability for payment fell on the family, not on the individual himself.

The wealth of the Irakh lay in their cattle. In law all cattle belonged to the tribe and were vested in the Chief, but by custom every family was entitled to a share. As a protection against theft the Irakh family locked itself in with its cattle at night.

If there were ever a nuclear war the Irakh would be prepared for it, because they make their homes in the bowels of the hills. They tunnel deep, and support the roof with timbers, as in a coal mine. The interior is divided into cubicles of which some are stalls for the livestock and others living quarters for the family. Some of the homes I saw penetrated thirty yards or more into the hillside, and I saw as many as fifty animals comfortably housed in their stalls immediately next to the quarters for the father, his wives and the children. The sexes were separated and each wife had her own cubicle. The main entrance was closed at night with a palisade of stout timbers, reminding me of the portcullis of an ancient castle. Such a habitation takes many months to complete, but the labour is well repaid by the resultant security.

The Barabaig occupied the southern section of the district right down to the Singida border. They were a tall people, proud of bearing and refined in feature, and like the Irakh, had no affinity with the Bantu races of Africa. They were Nilotic in origin, perhaps akin to the Watussi, but much prouder in bearing, and extremely brave. In manner they were frank and extrovert, and gave their views to me and others without hesitation. Like the Irakh, they counted their wealth in cattle, but, unlike them, they scorned all idea of manual labour. Not for them the hoe or the axe. If furrows were to be dug for watering cattle or trees felled for roadways, others must be found to do the work. The women, like the men, were tall and handsome, and carried themselves with grace. A Barabaig girl running seemed to move like a chamois or a gazelle.

In spite of their manifest wealth, the Barabaig of both sexes wore nothing more elaborate than bark cloth. The unmarried girls, like the Irakh, were naked above the waist; however, they wore a kind of bronze corset around the middle. This corset was finely wrought and was the work of skilled artificers whom I was never able to identify. It was a sign of virginity, and perhaps also served as a chastity belt.

The young girls, or perhaps their parents, were responsible for an obnoxious and bloodthirsty custom. A Barabaig girl would not accept a suitor unless he could produce the fingers and ears of a man he had killed in fight. The victim must, of course, be a member of another tribe. Usually he was to be found among strangers passing through the Barabaig country—the servant of a European traveller, incautiously wandering too far from his master's camp, could disappear without trace. African travellers who were aware of this custom took care to travel in large groups, but even this was not always a protection.

The practice was still fully alive when I came to the district, but as I was only there temporarily I made no attempt to grapple with it. B., the outgoing D.C., was extremely nervous about visiting the tribe, and only did so with a strong armed police guard. On one occasion he brought a company of the King's African Rifles and made them give a display of rapid rifle fire to impress the tribesmen. Some of the Barabaig men told me afterwards that they enjoyed the 'fireworks' and believed that they had been laid on for their entertainment. Russell and I, who made this trip together, took with us only two African policemen whose principal duty was to see to the safe handling of our loads, but we warned our servants not to wander outside the camp.

Despite their bloodthirsty habits, I could not but admire the independent character and devil-may-care bearing of these immensely attractive people. I grew quite friendly with the maidens of the tribe and for the fun of the thing joined, at their invitation, in one of their betrothal dances. In these dances the girl would approach the man of her choice and thus show her favour. This was a hint to him to go off into the countryside and qualify for her love by despatching an opponent in fight. I, happily, was spared this challenge.

My first and most lasting impression of the Barabaig was that their social organisation did not fit in with our conception of naive administration. There was no cohesive factor in their system; they were simply a collection of independent families who conducted their own affairs and had no call for any organised form of government. Their habits were nomadic, because of the need to find water and pasturage for their cattle. They had no permanent villages or other form of settlement. Each family lived with its cattle in a circular kraal constructed of thorn bush — protection against lions and human marauders — which overhung towards the centre to provide shelter. The length of time a family stayed in a particular kraal depended on circumstances: when the grazing was exhausted or the water pools were dry they moved on. By custom, however, the kraal they left was theirs, and was left vacant against their next return to the area.

Some time later I tried a Barabaig on a charge of murder. His kraal had been raided one night by a gang whose felonious intent was obvious. He shot at the raiders with bow and arrow and killed one of them. I asked him if, at the time he shot the fatal arrow, he was in fear of his life. He replied that he was. I discharged him at once.

The Barabaig mode of living posed many administrative problems. If water supplies were to be organised on a permanent basis in any one region, there would be a danger of overstocking and overgrazing, however scientifically the water was distributed. If there were no permanent water supplies the nomadic habits of the people would continue and any form of organised administration would be unworkable.

The so-called Chief at the time of my visit was one Gejar (note the Hamitic name). Like his predecessors, he had been appointed at the behest of Government, but he was the sixth chief in four years, which alone indicated that there was no traditional basis for chieftainship among these people.

Russell and I pitched our first camp at Bassodesh within sight and sound of Lake Bassotu, the shores of which abounded in game, while its waters contained a herd of protected hippopotami. The first night in camp I listened to their deep-throated cries, like the grunting of ten thousand pigs in unison. From there we moved to the Chief's headquarters at Katesh. Our trip was on poor roads, but through magnificent scenery. At Katesh we camped on the broad moorlands from which rose the majestic 14,000-foot mountain of Hanang.

At Babati, in the Gorowa country, I witnessed a cattle auction. Several Europeans, including the Scottish earl, came from their shooting lodges and coffee estates for the occasion. It was an outing for them but all the buying was done by Somali traders. My journal records that 760 head of cattle were sold, and the Gorowa tax returns benefited accordingly.

From Babati we came to Dongobesh in the Irakh country, stayed there for two nights and then returned to Mbulu to await the arrival of B., the new District Commissioner. In a few days I would be free, I thought, to return to Korogwe. I had enjoyed two months of touring and sight-seeing, learning much about the habits and way of life of two tribes whose like I had not met before during my years in Africa. I had not, however, neglected the ordinary tasks of administration. At the risk of seeming priggish, I have to say that I never enjoyed being idle, especially in the context of my own job; therefore, during my travels I performed the normal duties of conferring with chiefs and headmen, checking the work of the Native Courts, hearing appeals, looking into the problems of the tribesmen and studying the tax situation.

Except among the Wambugwe there should have been no tax problems in a District richly endowed with cattle, in which every family had a share; yet, as in my previous districts, I found hundreds of tax defaulters. As well as dealing with these, I also cleared a lot of old people off the registers by giving them exemption certificates. This is a delicate matter in a community where a doddering and feeble old man may own many head of cattle. These Africans were averse to selling their cattle for tax payment, and if they had to do so, picked out the oldest animals. My policy was that if a pater-familias had a large family of sons and grandsons paying tax to the extent that there might be a hundred shillings or more coming out of one household, I deemed it just and equitable to exempt him. In every case I would first consult the chief.

As for the youthful defaulters, there were many bad roads to be repaired, and their labour was welcome. With Russell's help I marshalled them into gangs and distributed them where the need was greatest. The road from Karatu to Mbulu was the first prior-ity and received most of the labour. I found an old German settler named Siedentoff to superivise the work. He and his wife had been living at Mbulu for the previous eleven years, running a small hotel which gave them a bare subsistence. He was an architect by profession, which was especially suitable as there was a stone bridge to be built for which money had been voted. Some 12 miles nearer to Karatu another bridge was being built under contract by a Russian. All this work was started at least one month before B. was due to arrive, and he was thus spared some of the travelling hazards I had endured.

On 14 June 1935, B. arrived. When I met him on that day he asked me to postpone the handing over until the following day. On the 15th he said he was not feeling well enough to take over.

He had returned from leave without his wife, and I gathered from some of his remarks that he was fretting for her. Meanwhile I went ahead with the preparation of the necessary papers. On the morning of the 16th we began take-over proceedings, but after lunch he came to the office looking ill and with a pulse-rate of 120. We had no doctor to give him treatment, and so Russell and I decided that he must be taken back to Arusha. By this time he had become very weak, and in the afternoon Mr and Mrs Russell, with B. bearing a letter from me to the Provincial Commissioner, set off for Arusha. I stayed behind to await developments, but only on July 5 did I receive definite news of my future movements, in the form of a letter from the Provincial Commissioner at Tanga thanking me for my services at Korogwe and saying that I would not be returning there. A few days later I was confirmed in the substantive post of District Commissioner, Mbulu.

9

MBULU—THE SECOND PHASE

Having ceased to be the caretaker I now had to concentrate on full-time administration as the substantive District Commissioner. I did not foresee that my stay was to be short. Had I been prophetically gifted I might have tempered my zeal.

Having no lack of tax defaulters to supply the labour, I carried on the rebuilding of the principal district roads, and within a few months these were in a reasonable condition, especially the road to Arusha via Karatu. Before I left the District I could travel at 25 miles per hour on this highway without hazard; in Africa at that time, this was a good speed.

We now had the problem of constructing new quarters for myself and the forestry officer, and a new rest camp. Russell lived above the District Office, a stout fort-like German structure of stone, so he and his wife were adequately housed. My bungalow and that of the forestry officer were on the verge of collapse, thanks to earthquakes which shook Mbulu every year usually in August. They lasted almost a month and their daily frequency, at four-hourly intervals or less, was disturbing. Local tradition associated them with Oldonyo Lengai, a slumbering volcano 80 miles away. We heard the earth tremors approaching from the distance, like the sound of an express train, getting louder as they drew nearer, and then felt the shock as they travelled beneath us, rocking buildings and everything else in their path. The District Office stood up to them well, but the walls of the two bungalows and the rest camp had cracks through which you could put your fist.

I was at lunch one day when I experienced my first earthquake. As the tremor passed through the bungalow the whole building shook, my table jumped about the floor and my food was scattered on the ground. My cook, a stranger like myself to these parts, rushed out of his kitchen onto the road in terror, to be greeted with raucous laughter by some Irakh tribesmen who were squatting there waiting to interview me.

As I was reading in bed one night, a sudden shock threw me to the floor and knocked down my oil lamp — which I was able to extinguish before it started a fire. I decided that the new buildings must be constructed of concrete blocks, and gave the supervisory work to the architect, Siedentoff. With the concrete blocks we had no more trouble with cracked walls.

The Wambugwe, who numbered about 3,000 families, lived in the flat and hot country east of and at the foot of the Rift Wall, between Madukani and Kiru. They posed four problems for us. They had grown 800 acres of cotton but were too lazy to pick it; they lived in an arid plain, in spite of having rich and well-watered land elsewhere at their disposal; they were heavily in arrears with their tax; and they were ruled, or rather misruled, by the Chief of the Gorowa.

As for the first problem, the cotton was of excellent quality but completely neglected. To remedy this I marshalled every available man and woman to do the picking, and contacted one Michaelakis, a Greek who owned a cotton ginnery at Iduli near Madukani, who made a firm agreement with me for the purchase of the cotton at current market prices. I also fixed market dates with him. In the end 150 tons were marketed for a yield of 30,000 shillings, which helped substantially to reduce the tax arrears, although there remained many youthful tax defaulters.

As for the question of administration, I had come to the conclusion, in the early days of my stewardship, that Chief Dodo's rule was not beneficial to this tribe, and I told him so. He was not pleased at the prospect of a change, because his present control of the Wambugwe gave him an additional salary from the Native Treasury. I discovered that there was a ruling clan still surviving among the Wambugwe, but that it had been reduced to obscurity. The surviving senior member of it was one Mgenge who — by tribal law, and subject to his acceptance by the elders — was the rightful chief. The elders gave their acceptance, and when the Provincial Commissioner attended a meeting of the tribe at Madukani in August, he agreed to Mgenge's appointment and to the establishment of a Native Authority with treasury and courts for the Wambugwe.

There remained the problem of settling the tribe in better living conditions In June, having received the necessary governmental sanction, I undertook the task of moving the majority of the people from the arid plains where they were living to the rich and well-watered country around Kisangaji. Here the Gichameda river was available to provide irrigation for thousands of acres. A few of the more progressive families were already enjoying these good conditions, but outside their cultivation the ground was buried under vegetation. It would be hard work clearing it, but this had to wait until after the cotton markets. When they were over I gave an order for 500 men to be assembled to do the clearing; they were to be reinforced by our youthful tax defaulters. The clearing fulfilled a double purpose: it provided ground for settlement, and opened a tsetse-free road for the Wambugwe to bring their cattle into Kisangaji and thence to the markets at Babati.

By early September enough ground had been cleared for the migration of 500 families to their new homes. I planned this by drawing up a list of 500 hut-owners by name and giving them a direct order to move into the new area, build their huts there and cultivate *shambas* (holdings). This I was enabled to do by the Native Authority Ordinance, which prescribed a penalty of three months' imprisonment for disobedience. The new chief, Mgenge, fully supported the policy and, thanks to his influence, it worked smoothly.

In time the tribesmen themselves came to recognise the benefits of the move, and before the end of September furrows were running from the Gichameda through the new *shambas* where maize and bananas were being planted. All this time there were locusts and hoppers in the country below the Rift Wall, but they looked a sickly lot and did not seem a threat to any crops. They also had air-borne enemies — hawks — which fed on the swarms.

The Barabaig, as we have seen, are cattle people; therefore, to promote their economic welfare, it was necessary to create conditions in which their cattle could thrive. Three factors were involved: the tsetse-fly, grazing and water.

On the borders of the Barabaig country were belts of the *glossina morsitans*, the tsetse-fly whose bite is fatal to cattle and horses. To create a large tsetse-free area where the cattle could graze freely without danger was the first consideration. (This was the primary reason for Russell's posting to Mbulu; he had been recruited to the administration from the Tsetse Reclamation Department. He had normal administrative duties, but his expert knowledge of tsetse elimination was invaluable to the Barabaig and Irakh.)

The tactics employed were to clear thousands of acres at a time and then put in herds of cattle to destroy the undergrowth in which the fly bred. Such a policy worked best with a nomadic people like the Barabaig for whom movement meant no hardship, provided there was sufficient pasture and water for their animals. However, as the Barabaig were too proud to do manual labour, the clearing had to be done by alien Africans from a variety of tribes. The Irakh provided some of the gangs, while others were recruited from the Wanyaturu of neighbouring Singida who, being cattle owners themselves, profited by the work they did for others and for which they were paid. This made the operation costly, but this had to be faced if the people for whom it was undertaken were not prepared to offer a communal and voluntary effort.

Extensive clearings were carried out before and during my time around Bassodesh, the shores of Lake Bassotu, Giyeda Mog, Katesh and Dareda. Russell was the artificer of these achievements. I spent several days at different times walking with him around these fly clearings and was amazed by how much he had reclaimed almost alone. On him fell all the work of determining the areas to be cleared and the organisation and supervision of the working gangs. It was not possible, of course, to cover every piece of fly-infested ground because of the work-shy habits of the people, and there were Barabaig families who retreated from the fly into the Singida District with their cattle, thus creating difficulties for the indigenous Wanyaturu. I managed by the end of September 1935 to bring about the return of these wanderers when the fly which they feared had been banished.

With the fly under control, the provision of grazing was not a serious problem. Pasturage was plentiful, and as the Barabaig were not a large tribe and lived in a sparsely populated country there was no danger, as in other cattle districts, of over-grazing.

Water was our greatest worry. The broad and beautiful Barabaig moorlands had little of it, yet near the cedar-crowned summit of Hanang were abundant springs and limitless supplies of the precious liquid. In June I made my ascent of the mountain. The climb was gradual if strenuous, and from midway to the summit the mountain was covered by a cedar forest that was protected by law. Cattle were not allowed to graze there. Near the top and in many different places all over the mountain were deep springs of water which flowed a short way down the slopes and never reached the plain below, simply disappearing into the porous volcanic crust of the mountain and passing through subterranean channels to points of emergence 80 or more miles away. Some rivers in the Arusha District originated in the springs of Hanang, to the profit of its peoples and the depriva-tion of the Barabaig. The solution to this problem was to dam each spring and bring the water down by a contour furrow to the bottom, and then to built troughs along its line. A rough dam was built on one spring and a furrow dug on a gradual slope. The furrow needed to have a bed of stone to avoid washaways. There was plenty of stone, and the water was brought down successfully.

Until the troughs could be built, the water was led into the crater of an old and long inactive volcano, and thus was created a lake of several thousand square yards which provided for the needs of hundreds of cattle. This makeshift plan was all that could be done at the time, and it created conditions we feared—namely the stripping bare of a large area of territory around the lake shore. Later, when money became available, concrete troughs were built at intervals between the mountain base and the lake to relieve the over-concentra-tion. Nevertheless the Barabaig were not over—careful to preserve the new water supply that had been provided for them. Their cattle damaged the walls of the furrow, and I had to compel them, whether they liked the labour or not, to erect thorn fencing on both sides along its total length with their own hands.

This catered for the needs of one locality only. To the north, east and west of Hanang, water was still in short supply. There were several springs on the mountain that could be tapped for these areas, but such a large programme would require expert surveys and, once these had been completed, money. When I went to Singida to arrange for the return of the Barabaig emigrants I met M., the surveyor who had travelled with me on that unpleasant first trip from Arusha to Mbulu. He was now surveying the Mbulu-Singida boundary. At my invitation he came to Katesh and climbed Hanang with me to look at the water position. From a rough examination he told me there was sufficient water on the mountain to feed over twenty small lakes of about the same size as the one we had already made, but that it would take him at least a month to survey the routes of the necessary contour furrows. There should, he said, be three main furrows to the lower reaches of the mountain, from which minor furrows would run to feed the lakes we wanted. I had visions of rivers in the Arusha district running dry if we took off so much water, and suggested that we should content ourselves for the time being with building one more dam and bringing down one more furrow. We should then assess the results of this operation before proceeding further. Limited development of this kind was urgently necessary, because cattle were already coming from all over to take advantage of our existing system and, if their numbers were uncontrolled, large areas of the surrounding country would be denuded of pasture.

While M. began his survey of Hanang on these lines, I explained the plan to the chief and tribesmen. As there was insufficient money in the Barabaig Native Treasury to finance the dam and furrow, I asked the people who would directly benefit from the plan if they would be prepared to put up the money by communal contribution. I explained that if they did not do so, they would have to wait many years for water. This argument failed to impress them, and there the matter lay. The scheme would have involved the sale of cattle, with which the Barabaig did not like parting. Before M.'s survey was completed I had left the district, and I never learned if my idea came to fruition.

The Barabaig had a school for their children at Katesh. It was maintained from Native Treasury funds, but the Government supplied one African teacher. There were twenty-two pupils on the roll, but when I visited the school only eleven were present. I was not surprised. The school-house contained just one room, which was open to all the elements. There was also a dormitory building, but it was never used. A school of this kind could only serve its immediate neighbourhood, and many structural alterations would have to be made if a reasonable attendance were to be maintained. The truth was that the Barabaig, a nomadic people, saw no virtue in their children being taught to read and write, and so were not prepared to support our educational policy.

While I was administering this area I achieved some notoriety from a case of considerable legal interest. It earned a headline in the London *Daily Mail*, because it cut across the principle of English law that a man who has been acquitted cannot be tried a second time for the same offence.

One night in July 1935 nine Wanyaturu tribesmen on their way home to Singida were attacked as they lay asleep in their camp near Lake Bassotu. Eight were bludgeoned or speared to death, but the ninth managed to escape and fled to the Chief's village, where he reported the murders. Chief Gejar, with commendable promptness, arrested the murderers, who were twelve in number, and brought them before me. Three of them were unwilling accomplices and gave evidence against the others — who as was clear, had been after the fearful bride-price of the ears and fingers of an enemy.

Thinking this evidence sufficient I committed nine of the accused for trial by the High Court, sitting at Arusha. To my consternation and that of the Chief, the High Court acquitted them all on the ground of insufficient evidence. To me it was unthinkable that these murderers should be allowed to go unpunished. I approached the Attorney-General of the Territory and obtained a ruling from him that the acquittal of the nine accused by a British court was no bar to their trial by their Native Court under the laws and customs of the tribe, it being understood that this second trial would be concerned only with the payment of blood money to the families of the murdered men. Armed with this ruling I assisted the Chief in re-arresting the nine murderers and had them brought to trial before the Native Court at Katesh. The relatives of the eight dead Wanyaturu had been summoned and were present in force. Over 6,000 tribesmen were also present, including 1,000 young women brought there by my express command. Also assembled were cattle from each of the murderers' families, which would represent the 'damages' or blood money to be paid if there were a conviction.

The court consisted of the Chief and the principal elders of the community. Its procedure was all the more interesting in that it conformed fully to tribal custom, and was in complete contrast to that of a British court. Each accused was required to plead under oath. Since no tribesman dared break the oath, his plea was bound to be truthful. The oath was administered after a small pit had been dug, in which the accused took his stand. A spear dipped in honey was then applied to his lips and he was asked if he were guilty of the murder or not. All nine pleaded guilty.

When judgment was pronounced declaring the number of beasts to be handed over by the guilty parties, the relatives of the dead Wanyaturu were summoned to take over the animals allotted to them. They were then escorted to the Singida border under an escort of police whom I had brought down specially for this purpose. All the senior Barabaig present, who strongly disapproved of the barbarous custom which had given rise to this trial, applauded the verdict and declared with one voice that this was the most effective way of putting an end to these murderous practices.

This, however, was not the end of the proceedings. Although tribal law had prescribed the traditional penalty, I pointed out to those present that under the verdict of the court the main burden of punishment had fallen on the families of the murderers and not on the murderers themselves. It was right and proper that they should suffer a direct punishment. So in the presence of the young women, on whom the meaning of the proceedings had not been lost, I had the nine young men stripped and flogged. This was an administrative act of doubtful legality, but it was highly effective.

The impression left on me by the Barabaig after nearly a year's experience of dealing with them was that as long as their existing way of life continued they would have a long way to go before achieving a workable Native Authority of their own, and in the meantime direct rule by the District Commissioner would serve their interests best. I wished my spell of duty with them could have been longer, but this was not to be.

The wealth of the Irakh also lay in cattle, but, unlike the Barabaig, they cultivated food on a large scale and even grew a sizeable acreage of wheat close to the Chief's headquarters. Their Native Authority, presided over by their Christian chief Michael, was one of the most progressive in the Territory. It was Michael himself who had started the wheat growing; he also organised the marketing of the crop, bargaining for a good price with the Arusha traders and distributing the proceeds equitably among the growers. In every other way, too, he worked for the good of his people and my only criticism of him would have been that he tended to be too severe in his punishment of wrongdoers, favouring our method of fine and imprisonment in preference to the traditional principle of retribution.

Being well educated, he kept himself up-to-date with events. At this time the Italians were invading Abyssinia, and I had some uncomfortable moments facing his inquiries as to why Great Britain, which claimed to be the friend of the Africans, was permitting Italian soldiers to attack and butcher Abyssinians. We worked well together. I enjoyed his confidence and he was genuinely sorry when I had to leave, especially as my going was linked with the efforts I had made to preserve the rights of his tribe *vis-à-vis* foreign planters.

As in the Barabaig country, our policy was directed towards maintaining the quality and health of cattle. Here reclamation of land from the tsetse-fly had made greater strides because the Irakh were willing workers. The reclamation progressed to the Kondoa boundary in the east (taking in all the Gorowa country), to the Serengeti plains in the north and to Lake Eyasi in the north-west. It could fairly be claimed that the whole of the Irakh country was fly-free, and Michael wished to keep it so by ensuring that all reclaimed country was quickly stocked with cattle.

The questions of pasturage and water did not hear the same aspect among the Irakh as among their Barabaig neighbours. The Irakh had a settled way of life, with homes tunnelled into the hills, and were not disposed to wander in search of grass and water. These needs had to be supplied as near to their habitations as possible. The water question, except in one important area, presented no real difficulty, but for that reason there was danger of overgrazing, which had already happened in some parts. The danger could be overcome if some families could be persuaded to move to places where there was abundant room and all conditions were favourable. One such place—Mbulumbul, north of Lake Manyara and east of the Ngorongoro creater—offered ample scope for expansion, and Michael wanted to settle 500 families there. This was magnificent country, plentifully supplied with water and entirely free of tsetse-fly. I visited it with Michael and Russell in late September. We were accompanied by Irakh headmen and by some senior Barabaig who, unlike the majority of their brothers, were keen on settling here under Michael's rule. A fair sprinkling of families, mixed Irakh and Barabaig, were already there, but fullscale settlement was impeded by a serious menace—the Masai who lived across the border and who were notorious for their habit of raiding neighbouring tribes and stealing their women and cattle. Indeed a few days before there had been a Masai raid. but the intruders had met with stout resistance and been driven off.

As I walked through this delectable country I came to a tree from which a Masai corpse hung by the neck. I asked a local Barabaig in our party how this had happened. He said that this Masai, out of rage and humiliation at the defeat of his friends, had committed suicide by hanging himself. I knew this to be absurd; nevertheless

I pretended to accept it, and we moved on. A few minutes later we came across the bodies of two more Masai slain in the raid.

Clearly these raiders had received a rough handling and had departed empty-handed, but the fact that one raid had been repulsed would not be sufficient encouragement for others to stake their future in a country so exposed to violence. There would have to be a substantial system of protection. Michael's proposal was that the Government should establish a police post of three men, whom he would reinforce with another manned by three tribal policemen. I agreed to submit this idea to my superiors, and meanwhile we set about selecting provisional sites for the police-posts. These were on high ground and commanded a wide view of the surrounding terrain; they were also close to a thick belt of forest on the eastern boundary through which rading parties would have to pass on their way to the settlements. From the positions we selected the raiders would be quickly spotted. Moreover if they succeeded in seizing any cattle they would have tremendous difficulty in taking the stolen animals through the forest.

I hoped that the proposal would be accepted by Government, for otherwise a splendid piece of country would go to waste. The Superintendent of Police supported it, but the Provincial Commissioner turned it down on the ground that the Irakh should look after themselves and not rely on the Government to protect them in a situation of this kind. His decision was short-sighted: if tribal police alone had been stationed in Mbulumbul and Masai raiders had been killed, there would have been an unholy row. Government police were necessary to control such a situation, and without them the project could not go ahead. Furthermore, to leave Mbulumbul unsettled or only partly settled was to invite the tsetse to return. The P. C.'s decision was a heavy blow to the Chief. If I had stayed for my full term in Mbulu we might have surmounted the difficulty by other means, but as I left a few months later, the scheme died a natural death.

While I was in this neighbourhood I made a trip to Lake Eyassi and in the woods nearby came across a group of pygmies for the second time. Like all pygmies they were forest dwellers, living on fish from the lake and wild game from within the forest; and like pygmies elsewhere were not required to pay tax. In this same region I came across an old German farm that had been abandoned two years earlier. There were the remains of a wattle-and-daub hut in which the farmer and his wife had lived, and high up in a nearby tree was a covered platform to which the couple had gone at night as a refuge from the elephants that frequently raided the farm. In the end they had given up the struggle and returned to civilisation, and the farm itself had reverted to the bush.

The most serious problem confronting the Irakh was connected with the German colony at Oldeani, the squatters to whom I have already referred. The country between Oldeani and Karatu was a long narrow plateau fringed on one side by hills and on the other by thick virgin forests. From these forests flowed the main river, the Ndero, on which the economic life of the region depended. In the hills were the coffee farms planted by Germans who had been given leasehold titles. On the plateau and in the surrounding countryside lived the Irakh with their cattle. It was the German farms which were taking most of the river water, leaving only a trickle for the indigenous inhabitants.

I had first come across the problem when Chief Michael took me to Oldeani in my caretaker days while I awaited B.'s arrival. I found from an inspection of the Water Board register that one of my predecessors had given permits to the Germans to tap the river in three places and bring furrows to their farms. These furrows were taking most of the river water. On 19 May I called a Water Board meeting at Karatu, at which the Germans agreed to extend the furrows from their farms back to the river. They also agreed to stop irrigation at 4 p.m. each day and not to re-start until 7 a.m. the following day. I had little faith in this plan, but there was not much else I could do. As a caretaker D. C. I could not cancel the existing permits. The proper course would have been to leave the final solution to B., but when it came about that I was to remain permanently at Mbulu, I determined to look at the problem again. By that time it was clear that the arrangement of 19 May had brought little or no improvement. In July I surveyed the Ndero river to its source in the virgin forest, and while doing so came upon some buffalo. Russell and Michael were with me. Near the crown of the forest, about half a mile above the highest of the German furrows, we found an admirable rocky site for the building of a concrete dam. My idea here, as at Hanang, was to dam the river by means of a barrage of reinforced concrete built into the rock, so designed as to give 75 per cent of the Ndero's water to the Irakh by means of a furrow running down through the forest to the plains below, leaving the balance of the water to the Germans. There was no money in the Irakh Native Treasury to finance this project, but the progressive and intelligent Michael said that his people would pay for it out of their own pockets. Assuming that the furrow were dug by voluntary unpaid labour, the cost would be 4,000 shillings or £200: 3,000 shillings would go on the barrage and 1,000 on troughs to be built along the line of the furrow in the plains. This low cost was based on the fact that all the labour, which would have represented another 6,000 shillings, would be free and voluntary. At the time it seemed to me ironical that the indigenous people should have to pay in cash and work to retrieve the water that was theirs by right. Where now were the principles of the Mandate?

I could not, of course, go ahead with the scheme without the Provincial Commissioner's approval. To the official mind it was highly irregular and contrary to Treasury protocol that a public project should be financed by private subscription and not through the formal channels. When the Provincial Commissioner came to visit me in August I took him over the ground and explained the position. I assured him that I would safeguard the money subscribed and make certain that it was properly spent. I succeeded in persuading him that speed was essential and that the Irakh were in serious difficulty over the watering of their cattle. I cited cases of Irakh cattleowners being compelled to pay tolls to German farmers for permission to water their livestock on German farms: they were thus paying for their own water of which they had been deprived by our administrative action. I finally reminded him of the basic principle of the Mandate that if there was a conflict of interest the rights of the indigenous peoples came first. After much discussion he agreed—verbally and not in writing—to my recommendations and gave me permission to go ahead. When I gave this news to the Chief he produced 1,000 shillings in a few days. I gave him a formal receipt and lodged the money in the District Treasury. In the first week of September I drew up a contract with another of the ex-architects living in the district for the construction of a reinforced concrete barrage on the site already chosen. Attention was given to every detail, including the strength of the concrete mixture and the type of reinforcing bars to be used. To ensure the correct fulfilment of the terms of the contract I sent Russell to camp on the site of the dam and supervise the contractor's work. Hundreds of young Irakh males gave their services free. By the end of the month the furrow had reached its final destination and the positions of the drinking troughs were determined. All this time the dam was rising fast on its rock foundation. It was being built in a curve to trap the maximum amount of water, and we reckoned that we would have an outflow of many thousands of gallons an hour in the furrow. This was three miles long, and we packed it with stone to prevent erosion. It was also fenced as a protection against animals, wild and tame.

Before the project was finished, but when its success was beyond doubt, I reported progress to the Provincial Commissioner in a letter dated 4 October. On 13 October, when work on the barrage was almost complete and water was already beginning to flow, I received a reply from him, ordering me to stop all work on the project and informing me that I had broken his instructions.

It was out of the question to stop the work, and after giving my letter deep consideration, I replied accordingly. My concluding words were that, as I appeared to have forfeited his confidence, I would prefer to be relieved of my charge of the District—which is what happened when he arrived on 17 October. Having seen the barrage and the furrow and the progress we had achieved he was obliged to approve the scheme, but he lost no time in informing me that I would be relieved at the end of the month by a new District Commissioner. The last official function we carried out together was to hold a Water Board meeting at Karatu to approve the erection of the barrage. I could see no need for this, as the water belonged by rights to the Irakh tribe. Why should they need a formal Water Board permit to use their own water? However we went through with the formality, and thereafter my sole concern was to prepare the handing-over to my successor.

Looking back I see that I made two mistakes which an older and wiser man would not have made: first I should not have reported progress on the project until it had been completed and proved, and secondly I should not have reacted as I did to my unmerited rebuke, but answered the Provincial Commissioner's letter tactfully. For some time after the 1914-18 war and the expulsion of the Germans from the Territory, officers of the occupying forces were recruited to fill the vacant administrative positions and they brought to their task the mentality of the parade ground. To question their orders or decisions, however justifiable such questioning might be, was regarded as gross insubordination. I should have realised this and accepted my spurious guilt quietly instead of letting my indignation take control. As it was, the incident more or less blighted any prospects I might have entertained of advancement in the Colonial Service.

On 3 November I was transferred to Moshi District in a subordinate capacity, although I was a substantive District Officer. On 20 November I received an official reprimand from the Governor's Secretariat, and my annual increment already overdue was held up. I asked for and was granted an interview with the Governor when he came to Moshi, but he, in the true tradition of military service, supported the senior man and I did my case more harm than good. I became ill as a result, and spent a fortnight in Moshi hospital. Finally at the end of December I was ordered to go on leave. On the night I sailed from Dar-es-Salaam I was informed that my increment would be restored and my seniority left intact. But more than nineteen months were to pass before I was given another District.

10

LINDI AGAIN

I did not return from home leave until October 1936, having contracted blood poisoning in both feet, the result of tramping over rough country during the previous tour and of my run-down condition. For three months I was confined to my bed or a chair. I had two operations, the first in Dublin, followed by a relapse when I tried to walk too soon, and the second in the Hospital for Tropical Diseases in London, after which I was gradually restored to health.

I was not surprised to find myself at Tanga again in a quasi-legal job involving pure office work. After the stormy end to my Mbulu stewardship, I had given up all hope of returning to district administration; it now seemed a matter of watching the calendar and ticking off the months and years until I had completed my statutory period of twenty years. There were still six years to run. There was a Government circular in force at the time permitting officers to apply for leave to retire before their full time after ten years of service. I was eligible to apply, and did so, but my application was turned down. I did not interpret the Secretariat's refusal as a compliment, and resigned myself to soldiering on.

In December 1936 I stole a few days to visit my old District of Korogwe, 61 miles by car from Tanga. It was the time of the cotton markets, and I was naturally interested to see what developments there might have been since Thomas and I had distributed the first cotton seeds there three years before. I was cheered by what I saw. Even if I were to play no further part in developing the African's economy, I could draw some comfort from the part I had played in the past.

From Korogwe I travelled up the Luengera to Mashewa, arriving unannounced to the delight of my old friend, Sub-Chief Ali. The picture that greeted me was a total contrast to what I had seen on my first visit years before. Over a thousand people were at the cotton market, brightly clad and looking prosperous, all with their loads of cotton. I was given a warm welcome. The Indian buyers told me that Mashewa had produced 200 tons, double the yield for the whole district in its first year.

In January 1937 I took another trip to the Luengera, this time to Daluni, and found there the same conditions as at Mashewa— hundreds of cotton growers all with large loads to sell and coming

from the market with well filled pockets. I met my old friend
Swynnerton, who told me that the cotton yield was now twenty
times that of 1934 and had brought many thousands of pounds to
the Wasambaa.

In mid-July 1937 I received the astonishing and welcome news
that I was being posted to Lindi as District Commissioner, and I
sailed there from Tanga by a coastal steamer. This was to be my
second tour in that coastal district. The outgoing D. C. was
Ashley Hubert Le Geyt, a Channel Islander of culture and wit.
Some of his court judgments and District reports made entertaining
reading.

Lindi District extended 120 miles to the Masasi border in the
west, and contained about 100 miles of the Indian Ocean coastline.
It was the Headquarters District of the Southern Province, which
covered the whole southern belt of Tanganyika Territory from the
Indian Ocean to Lake Nyasa in the west, and also contained the
districts of Mikindani (now Mtwara), Newala, Tunduru and
Songea.

The Provincial Commissioner, when I arrived, was Alfred
Kitching, a Cambridge rugby blue and a former English International forward. As a young schoolboy in 1913 a friend had taken
me to Lansdowne Road, Dublin, to see England playing Ireland
at rugby. In the English pack I recall a forward who was very
prominent in the line-outs and loose play. That forward was
Alfred Kitching. I reminded him of this match—to his great surprise
and pleasure. When I sat in his office on the first morning he showed
me a letter from the Administrative Secretary at Headquarters which
contained the sentence: "I am sorry to have to send Lumley to
you." Memories in the Secretariat were long and not always just,
and some of its staff were experts in giving dogs bad names.
Kitching said that this letter did not influence him in the slightest,
and indeed all through the tour we worked in the closest harmony.

One of Kitching's greatest services to the province was the all-
round reduction of African taxation to a level that the Africans
could afford. Far more money came in under the revised rates. It
was a timely reform because the province was not rich and had few
economic resources.

In the district of Lindi were many sisal estates, mostly along the
coast. As I have said, it had been German policy to develop East
Africa through European enterprise with Africans as the labour
pool. This policy was most easily exercised in the production of
sisal fibre, the best land for which was in the coastal regions where
the soil was light and sandy. Here the German administration took
little interest in African cash-crop production. To encourage

Africans to be primary producers, and so diminish the labour supply, would have been prejudicial to the interests of the sisal planters. Where the planter predominated the African was to be a wage-earner.

The estate proprietor paid an annual rental to the Government for his land, a practice which was continued throughout the period of our administration. It would not have been possible in law to challenge these German titles, and to clear the land of its sisal crop for the benefit of the African would have been a major and costly undertaking. The planters were secure in their property as long as they paid their rents.

Sisal, however, was a wasting asset. It exhausted the fertility of the soil. To maintain fertility extensive manuring was necessary, and few planters cared to incur this expense, especially as the market was competitive and prices fluctuated. Agricultural experts used to talk of sisal being 'mined' rather than cultivated. The planter's remedy for deterioration of his soil and crops through overworking of the land was simply to ask for more land. I had many of these applications; however, it was a rule of the Mandate that no additional land could be granted without the full and free consent of the Native Authority or the local Africans, and every application had to be examined on the spot. Where the additional land was of no interest to the indigenous people the application could be recommended, but not if any movement or disturbance of existing African residents were involved. In nearly every instance I advised the Native Authority against agreeing to a grant; yet it was over one of these applications that I eventually came a cropper.

One of the fundamental difficulties in all these cases was the absence of any formal survey at the time the land applied for was inspected; such a survey might not be made for months or even a year after the Authority had agreed the application, either in whole or in part. All we could do at the time was fix stakes in the ground to mark the limits of the land released to the applicant; but there was nothing to prevent a dishonest planter from moving these marks and enlarging the area before the surveyor arrived. This probably happened in one of the cases I examined with the Native Authority: it was after I had gone on leave, but I had to take the responsibility for it just the same. Since it was my policy always to lean against any grant of additional land I can think of no other explanation of how this particular planter obtained more land than the local Africans were willing to grant.

The labour position on the sisal estates was not as complicated as it had been in Korogwe. We had no irate planters complaining that they were short of workers because of cotton development.

Very few local Africans worked in sisal, most of the labour being
supplied by the Mawia and Mwera tribes from Mozambique, by
the Wangoni of Songea and by the Yao of Nyasaland. If wages were
low—as they were—we were not economically affected, since our
people did not depend upon the sisal estates for their tax money.

The average sisal planter had a peculiar attitude towards wages.
At this period the sisal market was beginning to recover from the
slump, but wages were still being held at the depressed level of the
early 1930s. Here the all-powerful hand of the Sisal Planters'
Association was felt. None of its members could increase wages
without its leave, and leave was not being granted. When I suggested to one planter that wages should be brought up to the pre-
slump level he replied that raising wages would do no good since
he would get no extra work out of his labourers. I had to point out to
him that the issue was not one of extra work but of the fairness or
otherwise of the existing wage-level for the work actually done. He
avoided answering the question.

The wage of an ordinary sisal worker—that is, a weeder or
cutter—up to 1929 varied between 15 and 18 shillings a month
or 50 cents a day. From 1930, when the slump in sisal prices began,
this wage was reduced to 12 shillings a month or 40 cents a day.
I should mention that the average African could feed himself
reasonably well for 10 cents a day, and of course he had no rents or
other charges to pay. Nevertheless, at the reduced rate little if
anything was left over for clothes and other sundries. A fair wage
would have been 18 shillings a month or 60 cents a day, but planters
were too much concerned with making up the leeway left by the
slump to give thought to the interests of their workers. In those days
I had no doubt that sisal cultivation was one of the uglier forms of
exploitation of a subject-race that had no proper representation.
Happily our own Africans were not involved, but those who came
from far away to work in sisal were entirely dependent on the wages
they earned to maintain themselves and their families.

Among the planters there were honourable exceptions. The
British manager of a sisal estate at Mkowe gave his labourers a
break from work and a substantial meal every morning at 10 o'clock
in place of increased wages. It was better than anything they could
have supplied for themselves, and it resulted in a more contented
labour force and a great increase in production.

A brief word should be said about the Mawia and Mwera from
Mozambique. These people were exceedingly primitive. Their
principal diet was snakes and lizards, which gives some idea of
their tribal environment. Their older women were 'duck-billed',
a disfiguration caused by piercing the upper lip and inserting a

block of wood. This was done in infancy, and as the woman grew older larger blocks of wood would be inserted from time to time. The effect was to make the upper lip protrude well beyond the lower and give the appearance of a duck's bill. The motive underlying this grotesque malformation was the desire of the men of these tribes to protect their women from capture by raiding enemies, particularly the Wangoni. To uglify their females was the greatest safeguard they could give them. Happily this custom was beginning to die out, thanks to the growing influence of Islam, and I saw very few examples of duck-billing among the younger girls.

In spite of their primitive habits, the Mawia were skilled carvers in wood, and some of their work was of beautiful design. I managed to secure, at great risk to the donor, a carving of a Mawia priest's mask which I left for safe keeping with my London outfitters. Their premises were destroyed during an air raid and this valuable curio was lost.

Sisal planters on the whole did not have a paternal attitude towards their workers. Most of the labour camps consisted of filthy and insanitary hovels. When I criticised conditions to estate managers I was met with the almost universal reply that the living conditions of these labourers at home were no better, if not worse. Unfortunately the labour laws of my day were vague on the housing and on other matters, and attempts to enforce them could usually be defeated by a clever lawyer. Furthermore, during the sisal slump we were counselled not to be too severe on planters, as their profits were barely enough to keep the industry going.

Industrial relations between employer and employed were unsatisfactory. Three months after my arrival in Lindi, a gang of 100 Wangoni labourers stopped work and marched from a nearby estate to my office. I sent for the manager and dealt with the men in his presence. After three hours of talk I managed to find the cause of the trouble, which was that their own headman had been dismissed and they had been put under a stranger who was not of their tribe. I advised the manager that the original headman should be reinstated, and the strikers went away satisfied. The manager had not acquainted himself with the facts of tribalism.

There were other forms of trouble, of the type one would expect when labourers from different tribes were employed on the same estate. I was spending Christmas of 1937 with Kitching on the far side of Lindi Bay when two Africans rushed into our camp shouting 'Bwana, men are being killed!'. The scene of the fracas was a sisal estate one hour's march away. When I reached it I found a large band of Mawia labourers at one end of their camp glowering with rage and full of fight. Facing them at the other end were twenty or thirty badly battered local Africans, mostly with bleeding head wounds. It transpired that one of the 'locals' had come to the camp on ordinary business but unfortunately at a time when the Mawia were holding a ritual dance under the supervision of their high priest, who was wearing his ceremonial mask. Now it is absolutely taboo for any stranger to approach a Mawia priest when he is masked, and this the unfortunate local did in all innocence. He was immediately attacked. His friends from a nearby village came to his rescue, and the result was a bloody riot.

Although I sympathised with the Mawia for the outrage to their customs, I had to arrest the ringleaders of the attack on the innocent villager because rioting of this kind could not be tolerated. The wives of the arrested men protested, and I was in some danger of being attacked myself until I told them that the detention of their husbands would be temporary and that they would be permitted to see them while in custody.

One morning in January 1938 the telephone rang in my office. It was a call from an estate 15 miles out. The manager begged me to send police urgently, as his Mawia labour, armed with spears and arrows, were about to attack the labourers on an adjoining estate and could not be restrained. I set out immediately with twenty-five police and an Indian police inspector. Fortunately we arrived in time to prevent a clash. The invading party retreated when they saw us and gave no trouble when we made some arrests.

The cause of the row was a woman, who had gone to the rival camp. This trouble could have been prevented if there had been proper communication between management and labour, but after the day's work was done labourers were left very much to their own devices. There were exceptions to this rule, and some managers took the trouble to understand their labour and study their problems, but most of the estates looked to the colonial administration to solve their difficulties for them.

Sickness took a heavy toll of up-country recruits brought to the coastal sisal plantations. Many of these men came from high altitudes, where there were no malarial mosquitoes, to the steamy climates of the lowlands where they were immediately exposed to fever infection. Having no natural immunity they died in alarming numbers. Frederick Crawford, who was now at Mbeya, mentioned in a letter to me the heavy casualities among labour recruited from his area to work in the Dar-es-Salaam region. Not only climate but change of diet contributed to this. Estates generally were not too scrupulous about the rations they provided; again there were honourable exceptions who took care of their labour and saw that they were given the right food but I knew of few cases where prophylactic treatment against fever was supplied, and it was seldom that a sisal estate saw a doctor.

The shortage of skilled medical attention was a defect, perhaps unavoidable, of our administration, and Africans in all walks of life suffered from it. A territory with a low revenue and a thin population could not finance a comprehensive medical service, and the estate labourer had to take his chance with the rest. However, there seemed to me no reason why the Planters' Association could not have organised its own medical service and even a few small hospitals in the main plantation areas. This was not done, and the ordinary labourer had to rely on the services of Government medical officers, who were always heavily overworked.

Some missions did their best to fill the gap. At Ndanda, inside the Masasi border, there was a German Catholic mission with a well-equipped hospital and a woman doctor, a nun named Sister Tecla whose fame was widespread. She treated Africans and Europeans alike. She was a shining example of what could be done for the Africans, but there was a limit to what she could achieve, and medical missions like that at Ndanda were few.

Of course, even if it had been feasible to send every sick estate labourer to the European hospital at Lindi the majority would have refused to go. The witch doctors were not kindly disposed to the European medicine men, and discouraged their fellow-tribesmen from cultivating them.

The indigenous Africans of the Lindi district were mostly of the Makonde tribe, but owing to coastal and Islamic influences had lost much of their tribal identity. There was also a strong mixture of Arab blood, for this district had been a place of concentrated Arab settlement for many generations. Several Arab families had pre-European titles to freehold land, and I was frequently called in to settle boundary disputes between them.

The Arab fraternity played an important part in the social set-up. For many centuries the East African littoral was under the sovereignty of the Sultans of Zanzibar, from Lamu in the north to the Ruvuma river in the south; Britain had continued paying rent to the Sultan for the coastal region of Kenya for several years after occupying the colony. The Arabs had formed many settlements along the coast, one of the most important being Kilwa, which has a magnificent natural harbour. This was one of the stages in the dhow traffic between African and Arabia. From other harbours along the coast, such as Lindi, Mikindani and Bagamoyo, the Sultan's emissaries conducted their lucrative trade in the slaves they obtained from the interior. It was no surprise, therefore, to find a strong Arab colony in Lindi and abundant signs that Arab blood had permeated widely through the local African community. The strength of Arab influence meant the domination of Islam over all other beliefs. There was a Native Administration of sorts which had been framed to satisfy the hereditary principle, but as it consisted of seventy separate and independent headmen it was thoroughly inefficient. To expect coherent action from so many independent units was like expecting a parliament to run a country without the aid of an executive cabinet.

Where there is no effective administration the people suffer. The extent of malnutrition came to light during the Second World War, when we found that a high percentage of recruited Africans failed to pass the medical tests. We had to build special camps for feeding them up; if we had not done so very few Africans would have been able to join the Forces. Among Lindi tribesmen this state of malnutrition manifested itself in malaria, yaws, dengue fever, tick fever and elephantiasis.

I made it one of my priorities to remove the old and the sick from the tax register. It was a defect of our system that many people paid tax who should have been exempted, and many administrative officers viewed applications for exemption with suspicion and disfavour. I made frequent journeys through the villages and called meetings wherever I camped for the chief purpose of taking the unfit and aged off the tax rolls so that we could concentrate on the younger element. At every meeting I saw ample evidence of ill health, not only the diseases already mentioned but also hernias and blindness through venereal infection. Rupture was one of the most frequent effects of malnutrition. I once met a case of double hernia on the road and took the sick man in my car to hospital.

All these untended cases of sickness reflected the quality of the Native Administration. In a properly run community these unfortunate people would have been given the option of hospital treatment if they had wanted it, because Lindi had a well equipped African hospital with a competent staff, supervised by a white medical officer.

The Lindi people drew their money from cotton, sesame (simsim) and copra. All three items were in steady production, and there was no need for the administrative campaigns I had conducted in other Districts. Here it was simply necessary to maintain a steady annual growth. Cotton was well established, and it was bought by the owners of the local ginnery. From sesame was extracted a marketable oil which was a popular cooking medium in certain parts of the world; I also knew it to be a serviceable lubricant for motor engines. As for copra, the dried husk of the coconut, Lindi had a dense concentration of coconut-palms and this product tied with cotton for the lead in exports. In May 1938 a thoughtless bureaucrat in the Agricultural Department advocated the prohibition of copra exports because of the decline in quality. Such a measure would have done immense damage to the economy of the District and probably provoked a riot. Happily we scotched it. The cause of the decline was due to the picking of unripe nuts: this practice was stopped by a well-conducted propaganda campaign and a system of grading.

The local economy was definitely sound and with proper encouragement could be expected to maintain an annual growth. As a result the Native Treasury was in a healthy financial condition and money was available for road improvements and the sinking of wells.

The marketing of our products was in the hands of the Indian commercial community. It was they who ran the ginnery and exported the sesame and copra. There were no Africans with enough business training and acumen to handle these or any other commodities. Our part was to see that proper prices were paid and that every transaction was in cash.

There was just one item of trade which was in African control all the way to the consumer — fish. Meat was unobtainable in Lindi, except when we could purchase it from a passing steamer, and fish was therefore the main source of protein for both black and white. It was caught by African sea-fishermen in small outrigger dug-out canoes.

At first we had trouble over the sale of fish. Although Lindi had a well constructed market, the fishermen preferred to hawk their wares around the town, getting a better price for their catch. This meant that fish was only obtained by those who were abroad early. I put a stop to this by issuing a formal order under the township authority making it compulsory for fish to be sold in the market.

Among the Makonde people succession, to both property and tribal headmanships, was matrilineal. A man's heir or successor was the eldest son of his eldest sister. If there were no sister, succession was traced through the nearest female relative. I have often asked myself why this matrilineal system is to be found in certain tribes. A tribe in Bukoba who followed it did not connect childbirth with sexual intercourse. It was their belief that the female conceived by an independent process — call it parthenogenesis — within her own body. This attitude towards conception could be one explanation of the matrilineal system; another could be the cynical proposition that 'it is a wise child who knows his own father'.

The traditional religion of many African tribes is ancestor worship, which explains the African's strong desire for male children: in his belief they are the most effective agents to minister to his needs when he has passed into the spirit world.

Those Africans in Lindi who were not converts to Islam or Christianity followed this traditional cult. The Makonde had an annual feast (*ngoma*) in honour of their dead every September. Its name was *Ziara*, and it was anything but mournful. Singing and dancing were its features: the participants believed that by these means they could impart energy and joy to their departed ones beyond the veil. Muslim missionaries do not discourage ancestor-worship, but harmonise it with their own teachings — which is one of the reasons why Islam has made headway among Africans. Every Muslim is a missionary, and because the Arab can achieve closer mental contact with the primitive African tribes than his European rival, Islam has made rapid strides wherever there are Arab settlements.

In the Colonial era too many white people were under the impression that the tribal African was a being utterly devoid of sensitivity or conscience. I had much proof of the contrary. One day in June 1938 an African came to my office and said that he wanted to confess to the murder of his wife. It appeared that she had been killed in the village of Natuno, three years before. He himself had disappeared, but his brother had given incriminating evidence against him. A few months later this brother had committed suicide. The alleged murderer told me that he had hidden for three years in Mozambique, but could endure his exile no longer. 'If I have to die', he said, 'I prefer to die in my own country.' He had killed his wife because she had been unfaithful to him and brought disgrace on the family.

I told him that there was no evidence against him and that he should think hard before asking me to record his confession. I then sent him away. The next day he returned, and I directed him to be sent to his Native Authority, who would find him a suitable place to live. A month later the Authority brought him back to me. They charged him with going berserk and setting fire to houses in the village where he had been sent to live. Clearly the memory of his wife's death had affected his mind. All that I could do was imprison him for arson and ask the medical officer to keep an eye on him. Imprisonment seemed to do the trick, because he gave no further trouble.

The trial of capital and other serious cases under extended jurisdiction from the High Court was always a bugbear, and it pursued me here. When I passed through Dar-es-Salaam on my way to Lindi I discussed the question with the High Court judges and told them of the strain that these trials imposed on a District Commissioner. They were sympathetic, but pointed out that they did not like coming to Lindi as there was no hotel there. (In fact one was being built on the shore, but it was not be ready until at least a year later.) So I became involved in the trial of three murder cases during my tour. In one I acquitted the accused; in the second I reduced the charge to manslaughter; only the third is worth recalling because of its consequences, which would only have been possible in an African territory.

The case involved two brothers, aged about twenty and twenty-four. One of them had been having affairs with two sisters. The elders of the girls' family were so outraged that they banned this Casanova from their village. He, not taking kindly to the ban, brought his brother with him to the girls' home and beat up an uncle so badly that he died. The murder weapon was a heavy stick resembling a knobkerry, and was wielded by the fornicator alone. His brother was unarmed.

I convicted Casanova of murder and, on the principle of constructive murder, convicted the brother of the same offence. Both were sentenced to death. The trial record was sent to the High Court and the sentence was confirmed. My next duty was to draft the usual report for the Governor on the convicted murderers, with my recommendation as to commutation of the sentence, or otherwise. The Native Authority view of the case, which had to be embodied in the report, was that both should be hanged. However, the report had to be withheld until an appeal had been heard or, if there were no appeal, the time for it had lapsed. Both men had already been advised of their right of appeal, and meanwhile were lodged in Lindi gaol awaiting transfer to Tabora for execution.

What happened next will no doubt amaze those who are accustomed only to the judicial procedures of Western communities. Here in Tanganyika we were dealing with people who had no access to expert legal advice. The two brothers expressed a wish to appeal, but who was available to draft the appeals? Only myself, the trial judge. It was not a task I enjoyed, but it was a good lesson for me in practising an objective appraisal of my own judgment. I spent two evenings drafting the appeals, a separate one for each man. I noted every possible point in the prisoners' favour, and then took the finished documents to the gaol for their thumb-marks. I did not attempt to explain to them the points I had raised, because this would have been quite beyond their understanding. The upshot was that Casanova's sentence was reduced to manslaughter and his brother's conviction was quashed. My draft report to the Governor was torn up.

The main road from Lindi to Songea running through Masasi and Tunduru was the concern of the Central Government and maintained by the Public Works Department from Territorial funds. This was the road on which I had made that adventurous journey seven years before, when it took me seven days to go from Tunduru to Lindi. I had occasion to travel it again in December 1937 to discuss staff problems with the District Commissioner of Songea. This officer was clamouring for extra staff, although his predecessor had managed with the existing establishment. He had convinced himself that the dignity of his position demanded an enlarged personnel. It was my task to inform him that his additional staff requirements could only be satisfied at my expense, and that I was not inclined to co-operate. Our meeting was not cordial, but no more was heard of the subject.

The trip had a nostalgic element, because I passed through Tunduru where I had been posted for famine duty in 1930. The present D.C. was Stanley Walden, who had been a cadet in Lindi while I was handling the Tunduru famine. He welcomed me hospitably, as did many of the clerks in the District office. Walden had made some remarkable improvements. The shabby old D.C.'s quarters of my day had been replaced by an opulent red-brick mansion of his own design, with neat lawns and terraces surrounding it. He was now busy with building new District offices and police lines.

The district roads in Lindi were, of course, the D.C.'s concern. They were in poor shape, despite the need for suitable outlets for the cotton and other cash crops of the African population. With Kitching's help I was able to supplement the Road Fund with a substantial contribution from our fairly wealthy Native Treasury, and, with the added asset of tax defaulters, organised a feasible road improvement programme. In accordance with my established policy I put the road gangs under reliable European supervision, which ensured that the labourers would be properly fed and their health adequately protected.

Of the two Europeans I employed, one was a German Jew, D., who had recently lost his job as assistant manager on a sisal estate because of staff reductions; the fact that he was a Jew would not have been in his favour when work was tight. He had been a medical student in Germany when the Nazis had begun their persecution of Jews. He had been compelled to give up his studies and leave Germany, and now he was taking what work he could find in Tanganyika. One evening as I sat in his camp, with war two years away, he told me that if Germany went to war in Europe every Jew who came under the Nazis' control would be eliminated — a remarkable prophecy.

The second overseer was a Scotsman, Barker. One night over a drink, he told me the story of his life, which resembled that of a fifteenth-century *condottiere*. At eighteen he left Scotland for California where he tried unsuccessfully to grow vines. When the Cuban-Spanish war broke out he went to fight for the Cubans. After that, he tried wheat-growing in Canada, but that was not a success, and so a year later he jumped at the opportunity of going to South Africa with Strathcona's Horse. There he was one of a band of 200 selected to dash through Mozambique and blow up the main bridge on the Beira railway, thus preventing ammunition reaching the Boers by that route, but the venture failed. He ended the Boer War as a member of Buller's column on the left wing of Roberts's march to Pretoria. After the war he joined a police force for duty on the Swaziland-Portuguese border. When the Great War broke out in 1914 he fought under Louis Botha in German South-West Africa; his story of the cavalry march across the desert to nip De Wet's rebellion in the bud was enthralling in itself. At the end of this campaign, still thirsting for action, Barker went north with the King's African Rifles to fight under Smuts in German East Africa. After that campaign he could have obtained a post in the administration, as did many of his comrades, but not for Barker the tame life of a District Officer. Instead he turned to elephant-poaching on the Portuguese border, and when this dried up after 1930 he tried trading in tobacco with Africans on the Ruvuma. Then he went down with sleeping sickness, and, after an amazing recovery, decided to relinquish his life of a gentleman adventurer. Meanwhile he had narrowly escaped a long sojourn in a Portuguese gaol for killing an African. He had been displaying his shooting skill at an outdoor gathering of Europeans one evening, *à la* William Tell. The African was holding a board over his head and Barker was grouping rifle shots on it. It was late in the evening and getting dark. The African's arms grew tried and he let the board drop too low. Administration on the Portuguese side was not strict and an African's life was not valued highly.

I never knew anyone give more thought to his appearance than Barker, in spite of the roughness of his surroundings and the condiitons in which he worked. He would never sit down in the evening for his drink or meal until he had bathed and attired himself in spotless linen.

Both men did excellent work and got the best out of their labour without ill-using them. The cost of their salaries was more than justified by the results. When the time came for the cotton and copra markets we had a reasonable system of District roads.

Native Administration was the principal problem that Kitching and I had to face—and solve. In Lindi there was no tribal organisation on which to build. As in most coastal regions any tribal organisation that might have existed had broken down in the face of Arab occupation and the pressures of Islam. All that was left of traditional African society was a collection of some hundreds of independent villages, each a law unto itself. The only authority any village acknowledged was its own headman, whose position had come to him by matrilineal succession. Clearly we could not build an Indirect Rule organisation on a multiple Native Authority of this kind without some cohesive factor. The unifying amalgam which Government used was the artificial creation of superheadmen known as *wakulungwa* (singular *mkulungwa*), each of whom was given a group of villages. There were seventy of them altogether, and they constituted the Native Authority. They were supposed to meet in conference four times a year and formulate policy. But having no basis in tribal law, they had no real authority and the system never worked except on paper. The only function they performed with any regularity was the collection of their salaries from the Native Treasury every month. They were also good at pocketing tax money, and more than one of them served a sentence in Lindi gaol. Since they were quite incapable of performing the ordinary duties of administration or promoting agricultural campaigns a heavy burden was placed on the District Commissioner to ensure the wellbeing of the African population.

Kitching decided that the whole system of Indirect Rule must be reshaped in Lindi District and that some genuine cohesive factor must be found to bind these separate communities into an acceptable organisation. Because the vast majority of Africans in the district were Muslims and there was a sizeable mixture of Arab blood in their veins, his view was that we should find this unifying factor in Islam and use it as the basis of a new Native Administration. I fully agreed with him. His suggestion was to create a number of Muslim magistrates or *liwalis* (Arabic for 'governor') and give each one a defined area that would include a group of villages. The traditional rights of the individual village headmen would be acknowledged, but the *liwali* would be the supreme judicial and administrative executive for the area. Kitching proposed ten *liwalis* for the district, which meant that each '*liwaliate*' would contain thirty-five to forty villages. We would then have ten Native Authorities to deal with instead of seventy. The supreme Native Authority would be a council consisting of these ten *liwalis* plus one or two of the prominent Muslim *kadis* or *sheikhs*. I gave the scheme my fullest support. A similar system was already being organised in the district of Mikindani, south of us.

Before we could make any progress we had to win the approval first of the African population and then of the Government. My Assistant District Officers and I toured the District from end to end, held meetings at every important centre and carefully explained the suggested organisation to our audiences. Discussion was free and untrammelled. When the village headmen, mostly good Muslims, were satisfied that their traditional rights were not threatened, they joined with the rest of the people in giving our proposals their blessing. There was hardly a dissenting voice. At Lindi itself, at Sudi, Mingoyo, Ruangwa, Ruponda and elsewhere our ideas for a new native authority were enthusiastically received. I was able to report to Kitching a universal 'Yes' from the Africans to his plan for a Muslim administration.

We now had to submit this plan to the Government. Kitching asked me to address a memorandum to him which he would then forward with his comments. I produced a draft in which I explained that the present system of *wakulungwa* was corrupt and unpopular and that we proposed to replace it with an administration based on Islamic law and culture, to which the great majority of the people adhered. The new courts would apply the law of the Koran to Muslims and the tribal law to those who still followed the traditional customs. I emphasised that the proposed changes had received universal approval.

Kitching and I worked on the draft together for weeks until we had hammered it into a shape we believed would be acceptable to the Government. Kitching was anxious to have the scheme approved before the end of the year, as the new Native Treasury budgets were due to operate from 1 January, and it was now October. I signed the memorandum on 29 October and he despatched it the same day.

To our relief, Government gave its assent to our proposals in principle on 11 December, and it became my task in the new year to put them into effect. This involved defining the ten new areas and selecting the *liwalis* to administer them. The new men had to be acceptable to both the people and the Government. On 31 December all seventy *wakulungwa* were formally dismissed, but until every *liwali* was installed the district had to be administered directly from the District Office. For the next few months I and my two A.D.O.s travelled continuously, holding conferences and agreeing with the people on the boundaries of the new divisions. Each division was then invited to nominate the man it wished to have as its *liwali*, it being understood that all appointments would have to be acceptable to the leaders of the Muslim community before names were submitted to the Central Government. Two divisions gave me nominations, which were acceptable to the Muslim leaders, who themselves nominated the remaining eight. These selections were very welcome to me, because I did not want the personnel of the new administration to be regarded as my own nominees. All ten were men of education and standing, learned in the law and with a considerable stake in the District.

By the end of February 1938 every *liwali* had assumed duty in his division and the new system of Indirect Rule had begun to function. It started smoothly and soon the improvement in the management of African affairs became evident. The Native Courts began to work efficiently for the first time. Taxes were collected regularly. Crop production increased and the state of the roads became better. There was a new spirit in the District, and the administrative officer received a cordial welcome wherever he toured. In one village during a wet period an African offered me his hut because my tent was letting in the rain: this was an entirely new kind of experience for me.

The people now had an administration based on the law which they observed in their daily lives, and it was being administered by men who worshipped in the same mosques as themselves. Moreover, every administrative rule was strictly related to 'the Book'. The Koran enjoins submission to authority — especially if that authority is wielded by men of one's own faith, properly appointed. A Koranic system of law, in these particular circumstances, seemed to fulfil all the people's spiritual and social needs.

Some of the ceremonies I witnessed at the installation of *liwalis* were impressive and moving. After the *liwali* had been formally installed the hundreds of people present were led in prayer by their *mwalim* and Allah's blessing was asked for the new incumbent. I was told by my colleagues that similar ceremonies were enacted at every installation, and this was proof to me that we had been right in acknowledging, however belatedly, the spiritual power of Islam.

The missions, Roman Catholic and Anglican, did not take kindly to the new administration. In their view, a Christian government was openly assisting the progress of a rival faith. We could not accept this, because a system of administration that ignored or ran counter to the basic beliefs of the people could never function; indeed it might lead to unrest and even, if times became troubled, to revolt. Islam was always sensitive to the wiles of the proselytiser, and any impression that we of the administration might give that we were siding with the Christian missions would have lost us the trust of the people. For that reason I felt it right to refuse in mid-1938 an invitation from the Roman Catholic Bishop of Masasi to attend the opening of his new cathedral at Ndanda.

The last act of this administrative drama was the selection of a new headquarters for the supreme authority where it could function with dignity. With the new Provincial Commissioner, Kitching's relief while he was on leave, I chose a site overlooking the sea, where a building was to be erected containing a court, council chamber and Native Treasury office. Before it was completed, I had left on home leave in August 1938. I went with the contented feeling that a tour that had begun with little promise had ended more happily, and that I had helped to accomplish something worthwhile. I therefore felt entitled to think that my career in the service might thenceforward have a smoother passage and that previous adverse comments would be erased from my record. I was to be disappointed.

11

KIBEREGE

I flew home rather than travelling by sea, to see Bradman batting in an Oval test match. I thereby sacrificed three weeks of off-duty pay, as the sea voyage each way was counted as leave. Bradman broke his leg fielding on the second day of the match, so my sacrifice was to little purpose. But I got married. As I was now a senior District Officer with sixteen years' service I believed that the better part of my career lay ahead and that I could offer my wife reasonably good conditions of life. My incremental date had passed during my leave, but had not been accompanied by an increase in salary. I attached no importance to this at the time, ascribing it to someone's oversight in the Treasury. This interpretation proved over-optimistic.

When my wife and I arrived in the Territory in January 1939, the Government had two wedding-presents waiting for me. The first was the stoppage of my increments and the loss of seniority that went with it. The stoppage held for two years, and during this time many officers who had been my juniors, some even having served under me, went ahead of me in the promotion stakes. Some of them were later to become Provincial Commissioners. The reason given to me for this disciplinary action was that I had allowed an applicant for additional sisal land in Lindi to receive more than the Native Authority was willing to grant. Since I was refused permission to proceed to Lindi and examine the ground in question with the Native Authority concerned, I have never to this day accepted the justice of this punishment.

The second wedding-present was my posting as District Commissioner to the District of Ulanga, with headquarters at Kiberege. I was to relieve an administrative officer named Theodore Pike who had gone down with blackwater fever. Happily he had recovered and was now convalescing in Dar-es-Salaam. Years later, as Sir Theodore Pike, he was to be Governor of Somaliland.

I met him in Dar-es-Salaam, and he made no secret of the adverse conditions in Kiberege. He advised me to try and have the posting changed; I received similar advice from a friendly medical officer. Apparently this region and the Rufigi Valley which adjoined it were classed as the two most unhealthy Districts in the Territory, and were popularly referred to as 'penal settlements'. Ulanga contains the Kilombero river, which joins with the Ruaha river to become the Rufiji. All these river valleys in Central Africa were notorious for heat and malaria. Anyone suffering from frequent attacks of malaria was, the doctors believed, susceptible eventually to blackwater fever, a disease in which the kidneys become congested and the sufferer's urine turns dark red or almost black—hence the name.If the kidneys cannot be cleared, the system becomes poisoned and the patient dies. During the illness the patient is plied with liquids of a purgative tendency and his heart is stimulated with sips, only sips, of champagne. The chances of recovery at this time were 40 or 50 percent.

In spite of my forebodings I rejected Pike's advice and decided that I must go to Kiberege without comment. Ulanga was part of the Dar-es-Salaam Province and the Provincial Commissioner and I were not friendly. This was his last Province before retirement. Significantly the brake on my increments was not released until he left the service eighteen months later. On the very day that he sailed from the Territory the Gazette announced the increase in my salary. Although he was not in any way responsible for the original ban, I suspect that he opposed its lifting while I worked in his Province.

The District of Ulanga had originally been part of the Mahenge Province. Mahenge, situated on a plateau south of the Kilombero valley, and the headquarters of the Province, had also originally been the headquarters of the Ulanga District. When the Province disappeared in an administrative reshuffle, the headquarters of Ulanga were moved to Kiberege, and Mahenge itself became a sub-District of Ulanga. The District Commissioner at Kiberege was, therefore, responsible for the affairs of Mahenge and for the conduct of the Assistant District Officer stationed there. He had to take the rap if anything went wrong, although he was too remote to be able to control his subordinate's activities. There was no telephone link or other means of quick communication between the two places, and so I resolved to give my A.D.O. a free hand and not inflict upon him too many visits of inspection.

The entire District had an area of 6,000 square miles. Its northern boundary was the Ruaha river. On the western border were the Iringa and Njombe Districts and on the east the District of Liwale, now known as Nachingwea. I decided to concentrate my attention on the Ulanga valley, the name given to the basin of the Kilombero river and its tributaries.

The reason for moving the headquarters of the District from Mahenge to Kiberege was, I believe, because the then District Commissioner was more interested in studying African diet than in handling the mundane tasks of administration, and he had found that Kiberege, with its low-lying, disease-ridden valleys gave him more scope for his researches than the healthier environment of Mahenge. This officer's personal eccentricity had thus exposed his successors to the risks of living in this extremely hot and unhealthy spot.

Before his time, and before the existence of Kiberege as an administrative centre, there had been a sub-station at Mkasu, an isolated spot south of Malenyi and close to the Ruhuji river. It was soon after the death there in 1925 from blackwater fever of an A.D.O. named Latimer that a sub-station was opened at Kiberege.

I visited Mkasu in August 1939. The house which Latimer had built and in which he died had been taken over by a Benedictine mission. Latimer's grave was in the shade of a large tree and marked by a rough wooden cross. I pictured in my mind this unfortunate officer dying in this desolate spot, miles from medical aid and with only his African servants to nurse him. Altogether five administrative officers went down with blackwater fever in the Ulanga valley, but only Latimer died.

When I arrived at Kiberege with my wife one evening towards the end of January I appreciated for the first time the significance of the Government's second wedding-present. It is not my purpose to bemoan my treatment or cast myself in the role of an ill-used servant (all this is now *tempora acta*), but my picture of our work in the Colonial Service would be incomplete without a description of the conditions under which officers and their wives were some times required to live. Our house was a rude structure of mud and stone with a grass-covered roof. Under the grass was a basic roof of corrugated iron, but Pike had added the grass covering to mitigate the heat induced by the sun beating on the bare metal. In so doing he had unwittingly provided a home for rats. The grass roof was infested with them, and they were not shy about making their presence known.

We were having tea one afternoon when three rats came down from the roof and with complete aplomb sat on the floor and watched us before scampering away. From time to time we found dead rats in the cupboards and drawers in which we kept our clothes and even in the miniature piano we had brought with us. We had frequent rat hunts, but to little avail and eventually we obtained a cat. The rat population then began to decline.

The front walls of the house bulged outwards ominously, but they had been buttressed with two wooden poles. The living room, which ran the full length of the structure, was fully exposed to the sun's rays in the afternoon, when it could not be occupied. It was clear that we would have to build a protective verandah to give us essential shade: this we did immediately. The floors had a cracked and uneven cement covering, which harboured innumerable tropical pests. The whitewash on the walls had dark brown streaks due to moisture running down from the roof. The one welcome feature of this hovel was a mosquito-proof bedroom which Pike had added; otherwise sleep at night would have been impossible. From early evening the mosquitoes were active, and between February and March, before the rains, we were plagued by the sand-fly. No mosquito net would keep it out, and we had to smear our bodies with an antiseptic cream if we were not to be driven mad with the irritation of its bite. Happily it disappeared after the rains broke.

These were not our only ills. Some months after our arrival, I was awakened one night by a strange irritation in my nostrils. I switched on my electric torch, to find that our bed, the floor and the ceiling were black with an insect known in Africa as the *siafu* ant. The *siafu* travel in millions in columns of almost military precision, and nothing stands in their way. They invade houses in search of food or other insects and their bite is vicious; they have been known to kill large animals by getting inside their nostrils and smothering them. I awakened my wife and together we did the only thing possible—we fled the house and retreated to a dilapidated rest-camp nearby. There we spent the rest of the night on a rough camp bed.

The usual method of repelling the *siafu* is coal or wood ash, but we could not expect to find these in the middle of the night. By morning our servants had succeeded in driving out the invaders, but not before they had cleared our larder of sugar and any other loose comestibles. They had also cleared the place of any vermin that was around, so that their visit was not entirely without value.

A few weeks later, we had a second *siafu* invasion as big as the previous one and at the same hour of night, from which we again had to flee. This was the last straw, and I decided to send my wife to live at Mahenge, where there was an abundance of spare and well-appointed quarters.

Our 'house' at Kiberege was perched on a small hill overlooking a wide plain that stretched as far as the eye could see—it lay between the Ruaha and Kilombero rivers. In the hot season between October and March, shade temperatures at 2 p.m. reached 103 degrees and the station instruments recorded humidity of 88 per cent. A mile away, rising high above us, was a range of heavily forested hills, uninhabited except by game, which collected considerable moisture after the rains and had the effect, in the cooler weather, of causing a 40-degree drop in temperature for three or four hours after midnight. Although this meant cool nights for a five-month period between May and October, it also carried some danger to health.

One night, after my wife had gone to Mahenge, I awoke gasping for breath. I thought this was the end, and struggled in a desperate state to the edge of the bed. I then had the presence of mind to force myself to relax my body, making myself go limp like a yogi, and the attack gradually lessened in severity and finally passed. I was without any recourse to medical aid; my servants were asleep, and I had no strength to call them. I often wondered at the possible nature of this attack: was it asthmatic, caused by the sudden drop in temperature and the entrance of damp, cold air into my lungs after the hot air of the daytime? I cannot say, but the attack never recurred. In any case I dashed off on safari without delay, for a change of scene and to escape what I thought to be the noxious vapours of the forest.

While my wife was at Kiberege, we used to go for diversion to a tennis court of sorts below our hill, but during our first game we encountered yet another pest—this time the *sangaru* ant. The *sangaru* was not vicious but clung affectionately to the tennis ball. The ground on which the court was laid was riddled with these insects and after every rally and before either of us could serve, the ball had to be wiped clean. We had to be philosophical about all these nuisances—there was no escape from them.

When Pike had fallen ill, a young Assistant District Officer, C., took charge of the district to await my arrival. He was down with fever when I arrived and could not hand over to me for some days. Because of Pike's illness and C.'s inexperience, both the District and Native Treasury accounts were in a mess; in a variety of ways votes had been used for purposes other than those for which they were intended. Money from the road vote, for example, had been spent on repairs to buildings. No doubt these unorthodox expenditures were unavoidable, but I had no intention of 'carrying the can' for anyone else, and so I lost no time in calling for a Government auditor to be sent up to examine everything. C. took umbrage and said that I was accusing him of incompetence. When the auditor eventually arrived in April and called C. from his District for questioning, bad relations between us were aggravated further, but I was determined not to become involved in matters for which I bore no responsibility. Eventually things were straightened out to my satisfaction. There was never any suggestion of criminal conduct; it was simply that special funds had been milked for other purposes, and this was contrary to regulations. Knuckles that merited rapping were discreetly rapped, and there the matter ended.

I had still to meet H., the A.D.O. in charge of the sub-District of Mahenge. I had heard that he was a sick man, and a month or two later he left the District under doctor's orders and was replaced, against my wishes, by C., whom I have just mentioned. Both C. and H. committed suicide during the war—by which time both had been posted to other Districts. The long wartime spell of duty, unrelieved by home leave, imposed a nervous strain on all the officers in the service and several succumbed to it. Home leave had always been regarded as more than a rest from the labours of administration; it was also a mental relief from the pressures that would build on a white man working in a tropical climate. It has been estimated that between 1939 and 1945 the administrative staff in Tanganyika lost one-fifth of its personnel through death and illness.

After my take-over from C., and while the verandah was being erected at the front of our quarters, I thought it a good idea to pay a flying visit to Mahenge. My wife and I arrived there by car on 9 February. We crossed the Kilombero river by ferry and the journey was reasonably comfortable, but the steep climb up the Mahenge escarpment caused my engine to boil. We arrived safely and were hospitably greeted by H. and his wife. H.'s appearance confirmed the reports of his state of health; he was, in fact, suffering from amoebic dysentery. A few days later a telegram from headquarters sanctioned his return to England for treatment, and within a few weeks C. had taken his place.

I now had my first look at Mahenge. The contrast with Kiberege was staggering, and in fact such contrasts between places close together were typical of Tanganyika. The situation of Mahenge, on a narrow range of hills with an abundance of trees and rich vegetation, was pleasant, the air was fresh and cool, and mosquitoes were completely absent. Flowers and vegetables grew in abundance. As conditions were suitable for cattle, milk and meat were in good supply, and there was plenty of fresh food and fruit. It was strange that H. could not enjoy good health there, but he had probably picked up his infection in the valley country below the escarpment.

The buildings in Mahenge were up-to-date by local standards. The A.D.O. now lived in the former Provincial Commissioner's residence, and there were other houses once occupied by medical officers, Public Works engineers, foresters and other officials. Some of these were in danger of deteriorating because there was no staff to live in them. There was quite a passable concrete tennis court on which you could play, free from the attentions of *sangaru* ants. The administration buildings, in which the District Commissioner used to reside, were of the typical German structure—solid and fort-like— and erected on the highest point of Mahenge hill. The German *bomas* (District headquarters) were always built in commanding positions, for defence and to impress the local tribesmen. No African could fail to be conscious of the presence and watchfulness of the Ruling Power when he gazed up at these granite-like structures that were visible for miles around.

Mahenge was also the headquarters of a Roman Catholic Capuchin mission. There was a mission church, cathedral-like in its magnitude, also in an imposing position, with a capacity for nearly 2,000 people. It had been built by the lay brothers, one of whom was a qualified architect. To give practical effect to its Christian teaching the mission maintained a highly efficient medical service. The two doctors, a Swiss and his wife, ran what at one time had been the Government hospital. The husband did the clinical work, the wife ran the laboratory. This remote outpost was as well served medically by this highly efficient couple as any of the first-class Districts of the Territory.

I could not help contrasting the conditions at Mahenge with those in which my wife and I had to live in Kiberege. The subordinate officer had a properly constructed residence, with good amenities and services at his disposal, while I, the senior officer, who was responsible for the administration of the entire District, was expected to make do with a tumble-down shack in an oppressive and exhausting atmosphere with no amenities of any kind. When I returned to Kiberege I wrote to the Provincial Commissioner suggesting that my headquarters should be moved back to their original site. I was not surprised to receive a peremptory refusal. This verdict was upheld by the Governor of the Territory.

I wrote to Freddie Crawford, then in the Secretariat and on the ladder to a higher career, describing my lot. He replied with irony that it was not standard policy for Government to station its administrative officers in healthy places.

When I first arrived at Kiberege, I had a cadet named Peter Bleakley. His quarters were even more squalid than mine, and I tried to ease his burden by giving him as much safari as possible. I thought it hard on a cadet that a place like this should be his first taste of Africa. Happily for him, as I thought, an order transferring him to Kilosa came in March, but to my astonishment he was loath to leave. He liked the quiet of this place and was able to save some money.

In fact, the fewer Europeans there were on a station the better, for the reason that food was a difficulty. Neither meat nor fresh vegetables were available. We lived almost entirely out of tins. As there were no cattle there was no cow's milk. For milk we relied on the local goats. I had retained an affection for goats since the days of the Bugufi goat and the man-eating leopards. Goat's milk has a richness you do not find in cow's milk, and there is no cream like goats' cream for making cheese. Our African cook gave us many excellent cheese dishes from this source. The only natural protein available was in fish from the Kilombero. The most edible species was known locally as *berege* — a kind of perch. It has to be collected straight from the fishermen's nets at Ifakara on the river, 20 miles away, and then, because of the climate, carried by car at the highest speed possible to our quarters. This treat we enjoyed about twice a month in the dry weather; in the rains not at all. We had a refrigerator operated by paraffin, specially designed for tropical conditions where electric current was not available, and with its aid we could extend the fish diet to two or three days. Our tinned food, supplemented by wild tomatoes and spinach, was reminiscent of my Tunduru days. On my rare river safaris I shot a few wild duck, but this luxury could only be enjoyed in camp.

It is now time to turn from my own troubles to the affairs of Ulanga. I soon discovered that the local economy was top-heavy. The major crop was rice, which was certainly cultivated in quantity, but there was little evidence of reserve crops. The position was potentially dangerous, because rice had to fulfill the two roles of a food crop and a cash crop. In other words, rice that might have been held in reserve had to be sold to pay taxes. A prolonged rain failure would have produced the conditions I found in Bugufi. Happily the rain did not fail, and the people reaped a rice crop of several thousand tons.

I had no reliable information about the size of Ulanga's population. No proper records were kept, which was not surprising in view of the inadequate office space. The tax was at the reasonable level of 7 shillings a head, and the position had been relieved by the abolition of the plural wives tax. This tax had greatly retarded production by keeping surplus women outside the traditional tribal economy, and since all non-Christian Africans were polygamous, it was widely unpopular.

I was determined that the rice crop should be used for food only and that other crops, such as cotton, should be cultivated for tax purposes. To assist me in the campaign I had the services of a District foreman, a Scot of over sixty named McDougall. In spite of his age he was fit and full of energy, and gave me admirable help. McDougall was a man of strict integrity, whom the tribesmen liked and respected, giving him the complimentary title *mzee* (old man), a title they would have given to an elder of the tribe, and which in Kenya was bestowed on Kenyatta.

McDougall covered the entire Ulanga valley to see that the orders for increased planting were carried out, and advise the people.

The soil was good for cotton, and for reserve food crops I fell back on cassava and sweet potatoes. Cassava was recognised as the greatest anti-famine stand-by, and it has saved many a community from starvation. (It is the root crop from which we derive that well-known milk pudding constituent — tapioca.)

In pursuing our new agricultural policy we were up against various difficulties, the first of which, though not the most serious, was the laziness of the men in certain chiefdoms. These men left the women to do all the field-work — a survival from the days when attacks were expected from neighbouring tribes, and the women planted while the men mounted guard. Although the days of tribal raids were past, the habit survived and it was my job, assisted by the chiefs, to eradicate it. I did not hesitate, when the need arose, to require every chief to issue compulsory work orders under the Native Authority Ordinance, on pain of imprisonment.

The next difficulty was far more serious. The Selous Game Reserve (called after the famous hunter) was sited in Ulanga and its wild inhabitants were no respecters of boundaries. The Government had stationed at Mahenge a game ranger who controlled a team of African scouts. Eight of these men were allotted to my area. They must have been brave, for their duties put their lives in continual danger. Only their skill protected them. Without them I could not have called on the Africans of Ulanga to increase their crop production, as I would have been asking them to work hard to provide more food for elephants, buffalos and hippopotami.

On my trips through the District, and particularly on my river journeys, I was frequently met with appeals for help against wild animals. On such occasions the game scouts never failed me. At Utengule in May a scout shot a buffalo that was eating a rice crop. During the same month this man, Ibrahim, shot eight marauding elephants. May, when the rice crop was ripening, was the favourite month for the raids. Wherever I was camped on the river at night I heard an endless chorus of animal noises — the trumpeting of elephants, the grunting of hippo and the roaring of lions. All these animals menaced African life in one way or the other. While elephant and hippo paid attention to the crops, lions attacked sheep and goats — and men. This District was in the man-eating belt, as its inhabitants had been involved in the Maji-Maji rebellion (see page 14) and had suffered the same blood-letting as the other rebellious tribes.

In spite of their impressive achievements in crop protection, eight scouts were not enough. The game ranger supported me in asking for eight more, whose salaries the chiefs were ready to subsidise out of Native Treasury funds. The question was not resolved before the outbreak of war in September, when I was ordered to call in all the game scouts and reserve them for action against a human enemy. For a time — happily a short one — the Ulanga tribesmen were left to fend for themselves. When all enemy aliens in the Province had been interned the scouts were returned to their posts — but still their numbers were not enough to provide adequate protection for Ulanga cultivators.

The ultimate success of an increased crop campaign had to depend on the amount of support we received from the Native Authorities. There were six of these in the Ulanga Valley. At the bottom of the scale was Ndole of the Wandamba tribe, half-blind and a drug addict; then there was Salehe of Mofu, a compulsive drunkard, also given to drugs; Mpepo of the Wangoni was an idler and heavy drinker. It was chiefs of this low quality who provided the critics of Indirect Rule with their ammunition. It was clear that little co-operation could be expected from these three; only direct control of their areas would yield the results I wanted. I could ask the Government to depose them, but their successors might not be much better: in selecting any new chief we were bound by the hereditary system, and I knew of no individuals in the families of these chiefs who were suitable to succeed them. Before 1926 Ndole's tribe, the Wandamba, had been under the rule of the Wabena chiefs. When Indirect Rule was introduced in that year, undue reverence for the hereditary principle resulted in their being given their own Native Authority, although they had long enjoyed the beneficent conditions of Wabena administration. The Wabena overlordship was based on conquest which, in African eyes, outweighed all other considerations, and should have been maintained. Later, in my Ulanga stewardship, I applied to have Salehe and Ndole deposed. I received no ruling on Ndole, but Salehe's removal was approved just as I was about to leave: my last administrative act in the District was to inform this chief of the Government's decision.

The other three chiefs were of very different character. Two of them ruled the two sections of the Wambunga tribe, one with headquarters at Ifakara and the other at Kiberege. Both were named Hassani and, as their names indicate, were Muslims. Hassani of Ifakara was no dynamic personality, but he was sober and righteous and ruled his people justly. I could be sure that he would support our agricultural campaign to the best of his ability. He had a nervous temperament and was always suspicious that people were intriguing against him. He was particularly wary of Europeans. This was not surprising, since his father, his uncles and

an aunt had been executed by the Germans for their part in the
Maji-Maji rebellion.

Memories of those harsh days had also affected the attitude of
the sub-chiefs and elders. Many of them were anti-European and
reactionary, and openly hostile to my campaign. I obliged the chief
to dismiss two of them, which he was perfectly willing to do, only he
was afraid of the possible reaction. I also obliged him to promote to
the rank of sub-chief a Mbunga of considerable merit who would, I
knew, improve the efficiency of the tribe's administration. Hassani
resisted this man's promotion, fearing that he would intrigue against
him. I soothed his fears by making the new sub-chief sign a declaration in open court pledging his loyalty and that of his descendants
to the Chief for all time.

Living in an atmosphere of feuds and intrigue, perhaps imaginary,
Hassani would never touch any food that had not been cooked and
tasted by his wives. As he was a good Muslim and therefore a tee-
totaller, no one could poison his beer. His suspicious attitude
towards men in general made dealings with him difficult, but on the
whole our relations were friendly and I am satisfied that he trusted
me. In June 1939 I was able to congratulate him on being awarded
the King's Medal for African Chiefs, the highest award to which
an African chief could then aspire.

Hassani Nloahanje of Kiberege was a tiny man, hardly more than
five feet tall. He had an acute intelligence and ruled his people
with authority. Shortly after my arrival in the District he called on
me and in the course of our conversation I learned that he had
already anticipated my measures for improving the food supply. He
told me that before my coming to Kiberege, when there was a
danger of drought, he had assembled his council and devised measures
against possible famine. These were to compel all the people to
break ground in the river valleys and flood it by damming the
rivers so as to produce emergency crops. For his tribesmen there was
now no danger of a food shortage. He went on to discuss his position
as a chief. Like most African chiefs he was not an autocrat, but was
guided by a council consisting of the elders of the tribe (*wazee*).
These men held their position by heredity, and many of them
belonged to the chief's clan. The others were chief's followers, like
their fathers before them. According to Hassani — and this was a
widespread belief in Africa — wisdom ran in families. Just as the
ironsmith inherited his calling from his forbears, so political
sagacity was handed down from father to son. Whether or not we,
as Europeans, accepted this philosophy, it was the basis of tribal
institutions throughout those parts of the Territory where the tribal

system survived, and it worked. Until the early part of the nineteenth century the government of Great Britain was largely carried on by a small number of aristocratic families who between them exercised political power over the rest of the community. Was this not also the expression of inherited political wisdom, the underlying theory being that the ability to order the country's affairs had been conferred by Providence on a small and select group, marked off from the rest by the conditions of their birth? Preceding the rule of the aristocratic families we had the doctrine of the divine right of kings, the underlying principle of which was remarkably similar to that on which an African chief based his hereditary rights.

I could be confident that Chief Hassani Nloahanje would wholly support a campaign to promote the production of cotton and other ancillary crops, provided he was satisfied that the soil of his country was suitable. If it were not so, he would not hesitate to tell me. I could not help reflecting at the time that if he had been chief of the Warundi in Bugufi there would have been no famine. As a good Muslim he would have been immune to the chicanery of witch doctors.

The sixth of my chiefs, Towegale of the Wabena, was a man of exceptional ability and personality. This I was to realise fully when I journeyed up-river to visit his country some months later. He was a powerfully built man of middle height, the stature one would associate with the chief of a warrior tribe like the Wabena. It was the Wabena who supplied the bulk of Von Lettow Vorbeck's army in the German East African campaign of the Great War; and it was this army that resisted an allied force of four times its strength for four years. If this people could have wielded their pruning hooks as effectively as their spears, there would have been little fear of famine in their country.

At a chiefs' conference in April I stressed the ever-present fear of famine and the need for an increase in food production and in the variety of crops to be cultivated. In addition to rice we had to have cassava and sweet potatoes and, for cash purposes, cotton. Tribesmen who planted cotton would not need to sell their food for tax, and I informed the chiefs that every man who planted this crop would not be required to pay his tax until he had sold it. I would organise markets close to the growing areas so that cotton cultivators would have their cash sources near at hand. I exempted fishermen from cotton planting, but ordered each chief to supply me with a firm list of them; only those who caught fish for a living would be exempted. I then mentioned that it was my custom to travel widely in the District and that I would visit each chief's country within the next few weeks and hoped to see that the decisions of our conference were being put into effect.

One immediate and positive achievement of this conference was that all the six chiefs agreed to amalgamate their Native Treasuries into one. In August we met again in conference to discuss the budget of the new Treasury. Conferences on this subject were always of great interest to me, because they showed the way in which the minds of African chiefs worked. Some were statesmanlike in their approach and proposed schemes for the public good, such as expenditure on roads, a new school-house, game scouts or agricultural instructors. Others were frankly selfish and wanted items inserted that would be of personal profit to themselves. But a conference attended by Towegale and the two Hassanis could not fail to be productive of positive suggestions, and I spent two enjoyable days at Ifakara, where it was held, hammering out a budget that not only had to be approved by the Native Authorities and designed for the benefit of the tribes but conform with the rules of financial orthodoxy.

As for our crop campaign and my promise to visit all the chiefdoms, I had already travelled over that of Hassani Nloahanje. Here it was a case of preaching to the converted. I had also frequently visited the country of Hassani of Ifakara, which was only 20 miles from my office. Things were going smoothly there too, and the chief was co-operating as best as he could. The other four chiefdoms, in the basin of the Kilombero river, could only be reached by water, as it was now the rainy season and all the District roads were impassable. The furthest chiefdom, Towegale's Ubena, was 150 miles away.

For river travelling the Government had supplied the District Commissioner with a motor-boat capable of carrying twenty passengers and two boatmen. At this time however, and indeed throughout my spell in Kiberege, the shadow of approaching war hung over us. Coded telegrams frequently passed through Ifakara, our only telegraph office, and twice when I was on the point of embarking in my boat I was recalled to my headquarters because of some crisis. However, these delays enabled me to work with the Government auditor, who arrived in April, on putting the District and Native Treasury accounts in order.

At last, on 10 May, I was able to set off up-river. I did not take my wife with me the first time, as I had no idea of the camping conditions or what hardships might lie ahead. As all four chiefdoms were on tributaries of the main river, some of which were too shallow for the motor-boat, the timing of departure from each camping stage

was important. We planned to leave Ifakara at 7.30 a.m. but did
not get away until 9.30 a.m. because the road from the Chief's
village to the embarkation pier was flooded and we had to reach it
by canoe. I took McDougall with me, and in all we were seventeen
people with forty-six loads.

We reached our first camp Cha Moto ('the Place of the Camp
Fire') at 6 p.m. On the way we had seen one hippo, two crocodiles
and a small herd of elephants, with white birds perched on their backs
picking off the ticks. Guessing what conditions on the river would be
like, I had armed myself with a mosquito-proof tent which an Indian
tailor at Ifakara had fashioned out of narrow-meshed gauze. We
were indeed glad of it, as throughout the night we heard the mosquitoes buzzing outside the tent.

We sailed from Cha Moto next day at 7 a.m. After an hour's sail
we came to the Ruipa tributary, and went up it for two miles to the
point where Chief Salehe awaited us with dug-out canoes. I transferred most of our passengers to the canoes, and the motor-boat,
relieved of its heavy load, was sufficiently reduced in draught to
make the journey to Mofu, but only because at this particular time
the rains had increased the depth of the river.

On this day's journey we saw four crocodiles, one floating in
the river and like a big log, the other three sleeping at different
places on the bank. One was at least fifteen feet long.

For the last three miles into Mofu there were continuous rice
fields on either banks of the Ruipa but no other crops. The women
and children were in the fields guarding the rice from birds, but
there was no sign of any men: they, I later found, were taking their
ease in their villages. It was Korogwe all over again. Several weeks had
passed since the conference at Kiberege, and the Chief of Mofu had
done nothing to turn its decisions into action.

I decided to spend the 12th at Mofu. The Chief, his elders, the
tribesmen and the women were all summoned to a conference. I told
the men that they were a worthless and beer-sodden lot, and lived
off the labour of their women. I gave them a definite order to clear
certain blocks of bush without delay and plant cotton, cassava and
potatoes and told them that if they disobeyed imprisonment would
be their lot. To drive home the point I selected three men from the
assembled crowd and sentenced them to a term of imprisonment
for breach of the order to plant cassava that had already been
promulgated. I warned the others that I would return to Mofu to
see that my orders were obeyed.

The next day I left, taking the Chief with me. It was my plan to
bring him to Utengule and show him how Chief Towegale was
carrying out the campaign. He was, of course, late getting ready

for the journey, thus delaying us. We then negotiated the twists of the Ruipa back to the Kilombero and thence upstream. Our next camping stage should have been Kota Kota, but because of the late start we had to pitch our tents for the night at a fishing camp, Mbutu, to which we were guided by two Wandamba fishermen. The elder of these had caught ten fish: I bought eight of them and he gave me the remaining two as a present. Because it was late, we could not pitch the mosquito tent, and the night was made miserable by all kinds of flying insects. By putting a lamp some yards away in a basin of water we obtained some relief; nevertheless, every forkful of food had to be closely examined before being swallowed.

We left Mbutu next morning at the usual hour of 7 a.m. and passed Kota Kota on our way to Ngombo. There were rice-fields along the river, and I stopped the boat to talk to some of the people who were on guard, mostly women and children and a few old men. Again there was a complete absence of the younger males. Here the rice was grown in the silt carried down by the flood waters. I told my audience that their men would be expected to plant cotton on this land after the rice had been reaped.

By 6.30 p.m. in semi-darkness and as rain was beginning to fall, we reached Ngombo in the Wandamba country, and pitched our camp. The camp site was on the water's edge and surrounded by pools—a miserable-looking spot. Chief Ndole lived some miles away at Merera, and was not there to greet us. In the morning a ragged person describing himself as the local Wandamba sub-chief called on us, but had little to say. I told him that I would return in four days, when I would expect to see all the Wandamba sub-chiefs. From the other bank of the river came a Mbena sub-chief (one of Towegale's men), and I took him in the boat. The others of his party followed in a canoe.

From Ngombo the Kilombero assumes the name Mnyera. Seven hours of travel brought us to the Mpanga, a tributary, up which two hours of sailing would bring us to Utengule. Because of sandbanks and sunken tree-trunks the Mpanga was navigable by motor-boat only during the season of high water, so after a brief passage we transferred the passengers and half our loads to canoes. I then took on a local pilot, and under his direction we reached Utengule in the late afternoon. A month later we would have had to make the entire Mpanga trip by canoe.

Our journey up the Kilombero comprised five days of actual sailing, eleven to twelve hours a day. Twice I shot wild duck flying overhead; this gave some variety to our somewhat monotonous diet. Otherwise the journey was tiresome, and after sitting cramped in a boat for so many days I looked forward to stretching my legs on land.

Chief Towegale received us in the grand manner. The route to the camp was lined with men, women and children. The camp and the Chief's village were in complete contrast to the headquarters of the other riverine chiefs. Flowers and fruit trees abounded. The countyside bore all the marks of good husbandry. Along the river were well — tended rice — fields and smiling crowds.

The following day I took a walk of several miles with the Chief, and was greatly encouraged by what I saw. In addition to the extensive rice fields, every Mbena had planted cotton for his tax payment and other crops as a food reserve. Towegale had set a good example with a cotton *shamba* of 30 acres. His people had averaged about one acre per man, which was as good as I had ever seen. If the crop were fully picked, every grower could expect a cash return of 60 shillings. As his tax was only 7 shillings he would, by local standards, have a substantial surplus. On the economic side there were clearly no immediate problems in Ubena. McDougall and I had only to agree on an agricultural programme with the Chief and leave the rest to him.

On my second day I carried out the routine duties of checking the Native Treasury accounts, inspecting the court registers and hearing appeals. All this time I had Chief Salehe of Mofu with me, and spared no opportunity of showing him how a good chief looked after his people. If this was humiliation, it was well merited.

Towegale had built himself a spacious two-storey brick house. The contrast between it and the shack in which I lived was pathetic. I often wondered what he thought of a government that could house a senior officer so meanly. Nevertheless his demeanour towards me was one of unfailing courtesy and friendship.

In many conversations with him I felt that men of his type were mentally starved by the lack of an adequate news medium in their own language. His questions showed that he was eager to learn what was going on in other countries beyond his own. I felt that the Government might have shown more initiative in providing a Swahili newspaper that would give world news to inquiring Africans, but I also had an unhappy feeling at times that this kind of indirect censorship was deliberate policy. It might not have been considered suitable for Africans to know that we who preached tribal peace in Africa had our tribal conflicts in Europe. When war at length broke out, I am sure that few Africans had the remotest idea of its cause.

Talking with me one evening Towegale voiced the opinion that an infiltration of European blood into the African tribes would improve their quality. This theory of miscegenation of white and black was advanced thinking for an African chief.

After three days at Utengule, McDougall and I began our return journey early on the 19th. Towegale came with us on his way to Itumbika, where he had a rice-field. I parted with him at the motor-boat mooring, but not before he introduced to me his young son, Lindo, his successor-designate to the chieftainship.

By noon we reached Ngombo (our speed downstream being much quicker) and found the Wandamba chiefs awaiting us. After my experience at Utengule, there was little pleasure in a conference with this useless lot of drunken loafers. I could only reproach them for their idle habits and warn them of the consequences if they disregarded my orders for an intensive agricultural campaign. I spent the rest of the morning inspecting the court records, such as they were, and in hearing appeals. In the afternoon I went up-river to select a new site for the rice and cotton markets—to which in due course an access road would have to be built for dry-season transport. Tribesmen and their women along the banks gave me a friendly reception: they were indeed a sturdy and handsome people, in marked contrast to their chiefs. Here was good material for progress under efficient leadership. I wished that they could have been restored to their previous union with the Wabena.

My words at Mofu and my treatment of Chief Salehe had borne some fruit, because I found that the ground had been cleared as I had ordered and planting was going ahead. In the silt lands near the river I planned an experiment with cotton after the rice had been harvested. If this proved successful—and I was confident that it would—cotton could be planted in every part of the District.

On the evening of 22 May we were back in Ifakara, and, after a full day with Chief Hassani, I returned to Kiberege. My first official action on my return was to write to the Provincial Commissioner asking for the deposition of Chief Salehe and of Chief Ndole with all his sub-chiefs. Salehe I described as a compulsive drunkard; Ndole as semi-blind, unintelligent and a drug addict; his sub-chiefs as drunkards, drug addicts and of low intelligence. This was a fair description of some of the characters who were responsible for Indirect Rule among the Wandamba tribe. I recommended that the District Commissioner be appointed Chief of the Wandamba, a procedure permissible under the Native Authority Ordinance, with a view to building up a fresh administration. The deposition of Salehe was approved just before I left the district, but no reply was vouchsafed to my proposals for the Wandamba.

Having probed the snags of travelling on the Kilombero I took my wife on my next tour of the riverine chiefdoms, which began on 10 June. On the first day she was bitten on the arm by a tsetse-fly, and by night the arm had swollen to such a size that I took her back to Ifakara mission to have it dressed. In the morning the swelling had subsided a little, so we took a chance and set off again. We camped at the usual places and I carried out my inspections as before, taking good care to see that all planting orders were being obeyed—as they were.

We had one piece of excitement on the way. At Ngombo early in the morning of 14 June we went for a stroll while the servants were loading the boat. Suddenly I saw about seven lions facing us in the high grass about fifty yards away. I had my sporting rifle with me. I took aim at a large male in the centre of the pride, and fired. All the lions disappeared from view. By now it was time to return to the boat, as we had to make an early start, so I could not follow up the shot; but when we came back to Ngombo some days later I learned that I had killed the lion, the only one I ever shot in Africa.

The same evening we reached Utengule, again to be welcomed in style by Towegale and a large retinue. The women threw rice at our feet and at night there were dances in our honour. The chief paid us the compliment of putting two rooms on the upper floor of his house at our disposal, and there we lived for four days in conditions of comfort that we had not known since coming to Kiberege.

Towegale took a liking to my wife. She had taken the trouble to learn Swahili, which she spoke fluently. She conversed easily and naturally with black people, and did not talk down to them as so many white people were tempted to do. The Chief took her into places in his establishment where no male could enter, and introduced her to his twenty wives and eighteen of his children. As a present for the Chief my wife made a water colour painting of his house which he greatly appreciated. In return he gave her a sheep, which we took back to Kiberege.

Now the shadows of war were drawing nearer. The subject was of particular interest to myself and Towegale, because many of the Wabena warrior veterans who had fought under Von Lettow Vorbeck in the previous war were still alive and living in the Ubena country. Some of Vorbeck's officers had returned to the Territory after the war as planters and businessmen, and I was concerned lest the Wabena veterans might rally to these old leaders and create a formidable nuisance for our Government. I confided my thoughts to Towegale, but he assured me that they were under his full control and were completely loyal to the British; moreover, if war broke out and I had any difficulties with enemy aliens, I had only to send word and he would put a thousand spearmen at my disposal.

On our way home I spent the day at Ngombo with the semi-blind and often inebriated Ndole of Ndamba. I persuaded him after much argument to get rid of his drunken sub-chiefs and install younger and more reliable men. I warned him that these drunkards could drag him down with them, and he saw my point. After this I thought there might yet be hope of bringing some order into the Wandamba, but I did not stay long enough in Ulanga to see the results.

Our journey from Ngombo was marred by an unpleasant incident. The next port of call was Mofu, 5 miles up the Ruipa river. We reckoned on arriving there by 2 p.m. on 20 June, but did not arrive until 5 p.m. What made matters worse was that Chief Salehe did not expect us until the next day, so no canoes were there to meet us. The Ruipa was too shallow for our motor-boat's draught, and we could do nothing except camp on the river bank. Our problem was to find dry ground for the tents, as the verge was covered with thick damp vegetation. Eventually we found a patch that had been made bare by the trampling of hippo. While our servants were pitching the tents and the cook was trying to start a fire it was suggested to me that I should fire a few rounds with my rifle, to scare off any animals. This I did, although I did not hope that it could produce much result. But just as our cook had produced a meal a shout went up that a canoe was approaching, and to my astonishment a large canoe came round a bend in the river, followed by two others, with Chief Salehe's brother in the third. They had come in answer to the shots. Although we were faced with a canoe journey by night through 5 miles of water infested with hippos and crocodiles, we could not disappoint the people who had come to rescue us from our present uncomfortable plight. So we dismantled our tent, packed our loads into the canoes and set off up-river in the darkness, with only the light of a young moon to guide us. The 5-mile journey took three and a half hours. In places the water was too deep for the canoe poles to grip and the crews had to use the reeds to pull us along. All round us the hippos were grunting. We could also hear lions giving off their nightly roars and occasionally the snout of a crocodile would be seen on the surface. I sat with a rifle on my knees, but did not have to use it. My wife slept most of the way, from nervous exhaustion. I was vastly relieved when at last we reached the Mofu landing stage. We entered camp about 11 p.m. to find the tents already pitched and our beds ready. Our servants had gone ahead with the equipment in the first canoe and had worked hard to have everything prepared for our arrival. To our further surprise the valiant cook was keeping hot for us a meal of bacon and eggs.

The next day, after completing my routine work in the chief's court, I visited a Capuchin missionary nearby and told him of our adventure. When I mentioned the danger from hippos and crocodiles he said that our greatest danger was from snakes. According to him there were snakes that could travel on the surface of the water. They lurked in vegetation on the bank and were in the habit of slipping into canoes that passed at night.

In spite of previous reports that Chief Salehe had mended his ways I found no improvement in the affairs of Mofu and the bush was still uncleared. I now gave him a final warning that I would suspend him myself without waiting for Government sanction unless his people took an active part in the agricultural campaign, and that meanwhile I would withhold his salary until all the ground previously designated had been cleared. I pondered at the time why none of my predecessors had taken any steps to have this chief removed. It was unfair to the tribe to keep them under the rule of so incompetent and corrupt an Authority. He was not even in the direct line of succession, being only the nephew of the former chief, but the two persons with the prior claim to succeed had died mysterious deaths which savoured strongly of poisoning. Unfortunately these things were almost impossible to prove in such a community, where the aids of scientific investigation could not be invoked.

Whether I succeeded in getting rid of Salehe or not, I was determined that my policy of an expanding agricultural production should be carried out. With that end in view I posted my most reliable agricultural instructor to Mofu with power to enforce my planting orders village by village. Any disobedience or obstruction of these orders was to be reported to me without delay, and the offender punished. I also took the Chief aside and warned him that failure on his part to give my man full support would mean his being summoned to Kiberege and detained there indefinitely.

We were back at Ifakara by 23 June. Chief Hassani was still glowing with pride over his King's Medal. I spent the next day with him touring his area, and saw extensive cultivation of cotton and food crops everywhere.

I had now completed two tours of the Ulanga District by river, and was satisfied that, except in Mofu, the economic and food position was satisfactory and that the Ulanga peoples would make good money from their cotton crop provided we had the markets ready and the roads to feed them. The problem of roads now engaged my attention, and I was not to travel the river again.

The main road from the railhead at Kilosa to Kiberege, Ifakara and Mahenge, with the car ferry on the Kilombero at Ifakara, was the concern of the Public Works Department. The department employed as a foreman on this section McDougall's son, who operated from the Ruaha river bridge to Mahenge. My responsibility was the district road system. The road funds for the Ulanga and Kilosa

Districts were in the control of a road board which sat periodically at Kilosa. These road boards were a new government departure: each was responsible for all District roads in its area. Ulanga and Kilosa constituted one area, and our board held meetings at Kilosa twice a year, in May to allocate the available funds to the two District Commissioners and in August to prepare estimates of next year's requirements for submission to the Government.

I had attended the May meeting before starting on my first river trip and had received my allocation for the year. Membership of the Board included both officials and non-officials, the latter being mostly commercial men and planters. It was the Government's way of giving business an opportunity of sharing in general administration, especially in matters that concerned the commercial community. There was always a considerable tug-of-war between rival interests before the final grants were approved.

Happily for me there were no European planters in Ulanga. The tribes had the whole country to themselves, and I had only one set of interests to protect. Nevertheless the grants were never generous—in a Territory with a scattered population and a low overall revenue they could not be—and they barely sufficed to keep the roads open in the dry weather for the essential markets, so that from the allocation one had to make provision for the replacement of bridges washed away by the inevitable floods. We D.C.s had to consider ourselves lucky if we got as much as £2 a mile for road maintenance; if we succeeded in wangling £3 a mile, this was unbelievable good fortune. No wonder we used tax default labour as often as we could and reserved the money for paying their rations. I had about 250 miles of district roads and for this I succeeded in wheedling £600 out of the board. I had also road funds in the Native Treasuries. This gave me altogether about £800, and with a few hundred tax defaulters I hoped to produce some reasonable dry—weather highways.

Road work began at the end of May when the rains were fading out. There were two official District roads in Ulanga. One, 123 miles long, ran north and west of the Kilombero from Ifakara through Ruipa, Mgeta and Merera to Utengule. The other ran east of the Kilombero, taking off from the main Mahenge road at Lupiro and running through Rufiri and Mtimbira to Malinyi, a distance of about 90 miles. These were the main arteries for the flow of African produce, but they had to be supplemented by auxiliary roads if our Ulanga peoples were to be given accessible markets for the crops that I was pressing them to grow. So from Malyni I built links to Utengule, Ngombo and Kilosa, Mpepo's home; and from Ruipa on the western road I built a link to Mofu.

Nearly all our roads involved river crossings, but, as was usual, the bridges were only seasonal and had to be replaced every dry season. In rebuilding them that year I had invaluable help from the Capuchin lay brothers. These men, who were skilled artificers, took charge of all our bridges. I supplied the money and the labour; they the supervision and know-how. The missions' co-operation was not entirely altruistic, as they too needed easy communication between their many stations.

The bridge over the Lumeno was quite a large project. Had it been constructed by the Public Works Department with paid labour it would have cost all of £600. The Ifakara brothers built it for £100, and gave their own services free. This bridge had more than engineering troubles. The river was full of crocodiles and the brothers were concerned about the safety of the African labour. We largely solved this problem by blowing off charges of dynamite. As a secondary precaution I advised that ropes be laid across the river up-stream, of the bridge; crocodiles attack downstream, not against the current.

A new technique adopted by the mission brothers at all the bridge sites was to build at lower levels than in former years. This allowed the river waters when in spate to flow over the top and leave the pile-driven supports intact. With each subsequent dry season we were then faced only with the problem of replacing the decking. Until we invoked mission aid the bridge-supports had been sunk haphazardly; with the first flood of the wet season, they were away. Now I watched some of the brothers driving the piles with a home-made pile-driver anchored to a pontoon of dug-out canoes; these pile-driving units were masterpieces of improvisation, and were certainly effective. In all, five bridges were built by these men. Not only did the missions build our bridges but they supervised our road repairs, except for one stretch of 36 miles running northward from Utengule which I left to Towegale's care. By mid-July the roads were ready for the passage of the season's merchandise. The Capuchin mission in Ulanga, had long been established there. Its members were mostly Dutch or Swiss nationals. All were cultured men, with a wide knowledge of African affairs. Not surprisingly I enjoyed their company whenever duty permitted, although I did not share their religion. Their conversation was on a high intellectual level, and they shamed me with their fluent English.

The Capuchin mission's headquarters was at Mahenge, but most of the priests were in my part of the District, some in very isolated stations. At Kissawasawa, on the Kilosa road 5 miles from Kiberege, lived a priest for whom I had a friendly regard: he was a

Swiss, Father Guido. Whenever I had to go on safari and leave my
wife at Kiberege the good Father would keep in touch and make
sure that all was well with her. More than once he came to dine
with us, and I always kept for the occasion a bottle of champagne
out of the case I had brought from home. The Capuchin priests—
rightly—enjoyed good living, and always carried a stock of French
or Algerian wine. They believed that good food and good wine
were essential to bodily health in a country where so many diseases
abounded, and they were able to endure the rigours of a tropical
climate much better than their Anglican counterparts. The
Anglican clergy I have known thought it obligatory to lead a
Spartan life and to forswear such diabolical pleasures as alcohol.
Their diet too was meagre. They always impressed me as frail and
delicate, and it was no surprise that their sickness rate was high.
Possibly all this self-denial was due to the need for economy: the
Anglican missions were not unduly wealthy, whereas the Catholic
ones could draw on considerable resources.

Early in August 1939 I travelled the eastern Ulanga road from
Lupiro to Malinyi with the game ranger from Mahenge to study
the effect of game on crop production. Beyond Malinyi I had built
a link-road to Chief Mpepo's village, and it was off this road that
I diverged to visit Latimer's grave at Mkasu.

On the same road I met a German driving a lorry loaded with
rice. His wife was with him. He stopped to talk to me, and I noticed
how shrunken and wizened he was. The reason for this was that
some years earlier a wounded elephant had seized him, broken
nearly every bone in his body and then hurled him into the bush.
His African servants found him still alive, packed him in mud
where he lay, and built a hut around him for shelter. They kept
him in this mud plaster for three months and fed him with liquids
through a tube. His bones reset and he gradually recovered.

My purpose on this trip was to encourage and if necessary compel
people who were living in isolated settlements to concentrate in
larger villages. Otherwise it was difficult for the game scouts to
protect their crops. I came across plenty of elephant spoor, broken
huts and smashed banana plantations. To persuade these people
to change the habit of generations and live in organised settlements
instead of small family groups was never easy. Often compulsion
was the only way. I found, however, that if a motor road were built
linking the area with a market centre, people would often leave
their remoter habitations of their own accord, and settle along the
road. I hoped that this would now happen, and that a concentration of population could be effected without recourse to the law.
Much, however, would depend on the co-operation of the Native

Authorities; since the position was worst in the effete chiefdoms of Mpepo and Salehe I was not optimistic. If the chiefs had been concerned with protecting their people against animal raiding they could have organised closer settlement without my intervention. In spite of their preference for living alone, the families would obey their chief. If, however, he was indifferent to their needs, and preferred an indolent life, social unity was likely to disintegrate as individual families drifted into isolation. This was the case particularly with the Angoni and Wandamba tribes, but not in Ubena where Towegale had long understood the problem and had it firmly under control.

I decided to wait and see how far the Native Authorities were able to go in carrying out my wishes before I took any further actions. Meanwhile I made it clear to the chiefs and headmen that the game scouts would only be called on to serve the closely congregated communities within a given radius, and that all outside that radius must take their chance.

On the road near Malinyi the game ranger and I were joined to our surprise by the medical officer from Kilosa who was making one of his rare tours of inspection. There was an incident while he was with us which illustrated how great was the Africans' need of skilled medical treatment and how haphazard were their chances of getting it if they lived away from the beaten track. As we left Malinyi for Ngombo word came that a woman in a village nearby had fallen from the roof of her hut and broken her wrist. When we arrived we found the fracture to be a compound one with the bone protruding a couple of inches. The M.O. said that he could not attempt to set it without an anaesthetic, but where were we to find it in this remote region? Then a Mbena sub-chief told of a German Lutheran mission at Kipangu, 3 miles away, run by a European sister. I took the injured woman in my car, the M.O. following in his with the game ranger. It was a rough bush track, and we bumped along in low gear. At last we arrived at the mission, which consisted mostly of thatched huts, to find a very competent—looking German lady at work in her dispensary. There was a crowd of Africans at the door. It was injection day, and they had come from miles around to be injected for yaws, ulcers and other blood complaints. The Africans' faith in the needle made it the only weapon with which the Europeans could triumph over the witch doctor. This courageous woman had lived there alone for two years, spending the days in work and the evenings in reading and writing. She had a bottle of chloroform, which she handed to the doctor. While she continued with her injections we laid our patient on a rough bed. I acted as anaesthetist, and one whiff of chloroform was enough to put the woman to sleep. Her wrist was reset and splinted and all was well. But what would have happened to her if there had been no European medical officer nearby, and if the messenger from the woman's village had arrived at our camp ten minutes later? The incident bristled with 'ifs' but chance had favoured this woman. I reflected at the time that until we could build up a substantial African economy and thereby create larger revenues from which to finance extended medical services, thousands of Africans would remain deprived of the treatment they so urgently needed.

I found that some people were not as grateful as they might have been to the game scouts for the work they did to protect their crops and for the dangers they ran on their behalf. At Ngombo, Salehe's country, there was a scout named Rashid. In one and a half years he had shot no less than fifty elephants, yet the tribesmen whom he had protected had not bothered to build him a house, although they had been ordered by the administration to do so. At the time of my visit Rashid was living in squalor. I warned Salehe that if the scout's house were not completed within thirty days I would force him to build it with his own hands.

Our trip lasted a fortnight. We inspected and confirmed the location of every game scout after consultation with sub-chiefs, headmen and villagers throughout the valley. We had achieved positive results, and if we could not assure absolute protection for every acre planted we had made things as difficult as possible for the raiders. The game scouts were fewer than we needed, but we had to make do with the resources available, which called for careful planning. We used our cars only for travelling from one camp to the next. Thereafter our tours of inspection were carried out on foot, usually involving 15 to 20 miles of walking a day.

As I and the game ranger parted company at Lupiro on 18 August war was approaching fast, and we had the unhappy feeling, correct as it proved, that this might be our last safari together. When war started three weeks later the game ranger was transferred to Arusha for special duty and Ulanga was deprived of his services.

One way of learning about tribal law, apart from by conversation with Africans, was to study the Native Authority court registers. My experience was that Africans were not happy to be asked about their customs, as they felt that these were matters personal to themselves, and they became self-conscious under questioning. More often than not they would compose an answer that they thought would please the interrogator. In the Native Courts, however, where all hearings had to be in public, the true law was applied, and, although the cases tried might cover only a portion of tribal custom, that which they revealed could be accepted as genuine.

The reading of the court registers was one of my principal duties. Even if there were no appeal to me from a particular case I had to be satisfied that all cases had been properly tried. If there were anything that called for correction I could apply my powers of revision and if necessary quash the court's decision.

Laws are generally regarded as rules devised to protect the fabric of a society, and the principle underlying them indicates the type of society that a particular people wants. Thus different tribes adopted varying attitudes towards certain actions or activities. In original tribal law some tribes punished adultery with death, others with compensatory payments. Under our jurisdiction the harsher punishments were replaced by retribution in money or in kind. But underlying most of the customs one sensed a definite social contract between the individual and the heads of the tribe.

In the court books of Utengule there was a plethora of adultery cases. The traditional penalty for this offence was payment of compensation to the injured husband. This did not seem to limit its occurrence, and Chief Towegale was so concerned that he suggested giving the offender the additional penalty of a month's work on the roads. I agreed to this suggestion, provided the punishment were limited to those who were physically fit to endure it. I knew that cases of this kind could lead to abuse: for example, when the tax—collecting season was approaching it was not unknown for husbands, unwilling to part with their cotton or rice money, to turn their wives into temptresses of unwary Casanovas and with the resulting compensation meet their tax liabilities.

In the Ngombo court a woman failed in a suit for divorce. The court was correct in ruling that according to tribal law a wife could not get a divorce unless her husband assented. I upheld the court's judgment on appeal, to the anger of the appellant and her relatives who became so riotous that the courtroom had to be cleared. However unfair the rule might be in our eyes, it was not the function of a D.C. to use his appellate jurisdiction for the reform of African law. But if that law were altogether offensive according to civilised standards, the Native Authority would be required to cancel or amend it.

In the same court an adultery case resulted in the usual payment of compensation, but this time the union had resulted in the birth of a son. The adulterer successfully claimed the child on payment of a further sum of 10 shillings to the cuckolded husband. Again we see the chattel status of the woman; but we also see the importance attached to the birth of male children because of their role in ancestor worship.

Peeping Toms were not popular. In another court a man was fined 2 shillings for spying on women when they were bathing.

In the court of the Chief of Kiberege a man was fined for assaulting a woman. The court ruled that the woman was not his wife and, therefore, he had no right to beat her. In the same court a man sued another for abducting his wife. It was decided that the plaintiff could not claim damages as he had not yet paid the marriage dowry. In the law of many tribes a marriage was not valid until the dowry had been paid.

I now give an example of Chief Hassani Nloahanje's enlightened outlook. A young boy was suffering from ulcers, and because his father delayed bringing him to the dressing station, he was fined. I found no similar case in the court registers of the other chiefs, and yet there must have been similar instances of neglect.

From my inspection of Native Authority court registers generally I noticed that, apart from occasional wife-beating, there were scarcely any crimes of violence, and I do not recall having a single murder case during all the time I was in Ulanga. When I commented on this I was told that the Wambunga and their kindred tribes preferred to settle their quarrels by poison rather than blows; and crimes of poisoning were almost impossible to uncover.

By the end of August the missionaries with whom I discussed the world situation were convinced that war was imminent. The Provincial Commissioner paid me his one and only visit on 22 August but was recalled by telegram the next day. On the 24th I left Kiberege intending to meet my wife at Lupiro and take her on safari with me to eastern Ulanga. She was now living at Mahenge. But on the way to Ifakara I was met by a runner with a sheaf of telegrams and had to turn back, as my code book was in the safe at Kiberege. Since our only telegraph office was at Ifakara I decided to camp there indefinitely, and so I moved there on the 26th. From then until the outbreak of war of 3 September I stayed at Ifakara. The Father Superior of the mission put a room at my disposal, where I was able to work undisturbed decoding telegrams and coding my replies. With me I had a small police guard. The rest of the force remained at Kiberege under the charge of young McDougall, whom I had appointed a special constable. Every day there were shoals of telegrams, some saying that war was about to break out to be followed by others saying that the situation had eased.

One particular telegram brought some relief. It advised that the

Germans in the Territory had given an undertaking through their
Consul that they would not engage in any violent or subversive
activity. When I read this I thought of Towegale's Wabena war
veterans.

On 3 September, when the balloon finally went up, I received
instructions to collect all German nationals in my District for
internment. Excluded from this order were two Austrian priests
who lived and worked with Father Guido and the German woman
missionary who had supplied the chloroform for the operation at
Kipungu. This left one German to be interned—a man of sixty-one,
who was a veteran of the First World War and a pensioner of the
German Government. He was squatting in a mud hut at a remote
place called Monghula. When I arrived to collect him he had not
yet heard of the war. I came at 8 p.m. and found him in bed. He
told me that his pension barely covered his food and the wages for
one servant. He could not afford lamp oil and so went to bed at
6 o'clock every evening after his meal. He was very distressed to
hear that the Fuehrer had made a deal with the Bolsheviks. I took
him to Kiberege for the night, and gave him a drink and a meal.

Living close to me was a retired Rhodesian policeman called
Fairweather, also a veteran of the First War. He was about the
only man in our locality who rejoiced at the outbreak of the Second.
He had been gazetted as a captain in the King's African Rifles,
which he found a welcome change after years of vegetating in the
Ulanga bush. I handed over my internee to him. He conducted the
man to Kilosa, and was then given command of a squad of police
with the special duty of guarding the Ruaha bridge.

While I was camped at Ifakara I came across a most unusual
man. He was of the local Mbunga people, uneducated and a
paralytic. I met him as I went into the telegraph office on my first
morning. He was sitting on the ground beside the office door, his
back propped against the wall. As I was about to enter the office
to send off a code message he greeted me in English with the words
'Good morning, sir'. Not to be outdone in courtesy I replied in
English with a similar greeting. He then made a further remark
in English, very much to the point and again I replied, thinking
that he would now have reached the limit of his linguistic resources.
But to my amazement he continued to speak fluently in my language, and so involved did I become in talking to him that for a
while I forgot the original purpose of my visit to the telegraph
office. His English, if not grammatically exact, was fluent, and he
understood everything I said to him perfectly. I asked him if he had
been taught English at school. No, he had not been to school and
could neither read nor write. He had been paralysed for several

years and could not move without being helped. He had chosen the
telegraph office as a likely place to squat and appeal for the odd
coin from passers by. He had been doing this for a very long time,
and could not avoid overhearing the telegraph clerks sending
telephone messages in English. By constantly hearing English
spoken he had first picked up the sounds and then the meaning of
the language. I have heard English spoken by many distinguished
and educated foreigners, but none of them was more fluent or
free in expression than this illiterate man.

On 6 September an open telegram from the Provincial Commissioner gave me permission to resume my normal duties, whereupon I took my wife on the interrupted safari to eastern Ulanga.
It was to be my last in the District. My wife again suffered a tsetse
bite, this time on a foot which swelled up like her arm on the first
occasion, and made walking impossible for a day or two. We were
at Mtimbira at the time, where the good camp facilities and the
now cooler weather enabled her to lie up until the swelling subsided.
This gave me time to have a good look about the area, and I was
glad to see the men busy picking their cotton in preparation for
the following week's markets. They were gratified to learn from me
that owing to the war they would receive nearly double the price
that they had been promised at the beginning of the planting
season.

On 11 September we were at Malinyi when instructions came
to me by runner to report to Dar-es-Salaam for special duty as soon
as possible. That was the end of the safari. Next day my wife
returned to Mahenge while I went to Kiberege to prepare the
hand-over to my successor. On 16 September came a letter I have
already mentioned, saying that my recommendations for the deposition of Chief Salehe had been approved. As Salehe was already
living under my watchful eye in Kiberege there was no delay in
giving him this information and telling him that in no circumstances
could he return to Mofu. This was my last administrative act in
Ulanga, and I was obliged to leave to the new District Commissioner
the task of appointing Salehe's successor. On 21 September I left
for Dar-es-Salaam to take up my special duties, and was not to
return to the administration until early 1942.

12

BUKOBA

On 23 February 1942, twenty-nine months after leaving Ulanga, I returned to the administration and was posted to Bukoba on the west coast of Lake Victoria. Scenically Bukoba was the most pleasant District I had known. The District Office and the staff bungalows stood a few hundred yards from the lake shore. From my bungalow I could look out on the broad waters of Victoria. Half a mile out in the lake was a green island, in which I found a cave filled with human skulls. I never discovered whether it was a burial ground or a one-time place of execution. Nearer to the shore a school of protected hippo swam lazily. They were very tame and often came ashore to graze, ignoring any humans who might be relaxing by the lake. Behind my bungalow rose forest-clad hills, emerald from the generous rainfall, from which a river ran down to the lake. The climate was temperate, and the cool evening air ensured a good night's sleep. Rainfall was spread over nine months of the year. In the first six months the rain would begin precisely at 6 a.m., fall heavily until noon, and then stop. By 5 p.m. the tennis courts and golf course were in perfect condition.

But this rain had an unpleasant feature — the lightning storms that accompanied it. The island of skulls had a rocky centre, and the lightning would ricochet off it to the shore and would enter my house if I had not shut the door and windows facing the lake. Our veterinary officer was struck one morning as he shaved; although a glancing blow, it laid him up for several days.

I was not in charge of the Bukoba District, but a District Officer serving under the then D.C., Frederick Lake, a man considerably older than myself and a veteran of the 1914-18 war. Although I had been offered a District of my own, I deliberately chose this subordinate post on account of the comparatively civilised conditions of Bukoba. I had no desire to risk another Ulanga.

Lake and I worked in close harmony for many months until severe illness obliged him to go on sick leave. All home leave had been cancelled from the outbreak of war and most administrative officers were tied to their posts without respite for as long as seven years, which was three times the length of the normal pre-war tour. Officers had also to endure the greatly increased duties of wartime food rationing and price control, the recruitment of Africans for the

armed forces, the maintenance of camps for recruits and the payment
of allowances to their families. No additional staff was available;
on the contrary, the administrative personnel of the Territory was
reduced by the secondment of officers to undertake administration
in the occupied Italian colonies. It was not surprising that sickness
took its toll of the overworked service; Lake became one of
its victims.

From the administrative point of view Bukoba was one of the
show Districts of Tanganyika. It had a full complement of officials:
Public Works engineer, veterinary officer, forestry officer, agricultural
officer, medical officer. All it lacked was a resident magistrate —
whose work fell on the administrative staff.

In the context of Indirect Rule and economic development
Bukoba was supposed to set an example to all other Districts. The
people consisted of a variety of tribal units all closely related and
collectively named Wahaya or Bahaya. They numbered approximately half a million and were ruled by eight chiefs, each independent of the others. However, these chiefs maintained a common
treasury from which they and their staffs were paid and the normal
tribal services were financed. By the standards of the Territory,
the chiefs were highly paid: Chief Alfred Kalemera of Kianja
received £2,800 a year, as much in those days as a junior minister
in the British Government. Chief Petro of Ihangiro received £1,000 a
year. No chief was paid less than £300 a year, yet many complained
that they were not paid enough. A chief's salary was calculated
according to the value of the tribute he was believed to have received
in pre-European days; possibly the calculation may have tended
to be low. Many of us suspected that the chiefs were still receiving
unofficial tribute, possibly in kind. All of them lived in good style,
which was right and proper. They drove luxurious American cars.
The model popular with them in my time was the Hudson Super-
Six; my own modest Ford was not in the same class, and I always
felt like a poor relation when I went on my travels with a chief.

These potentates all lived in stately homes, which was also good.
I refer to them as palaces, for such they were in relation to the
dwellings of their subjects. In March 1942 Chief Daudi Rugomora
of Kanyangereko entertained me at Maruku, his headquarters. His
palace was built in tropical European style, and was very pleasant
to the eye. After taking me through its many well-appointed rooms
he entertained me to tea in his summer-house, a beautifully constructed *msonge* (hut), fashioned in the traditional style of the tribe.
The walls and supports were of stout timber and the ceiling was of
beautifully worked bamboo strips. Even the thatching of the roof
was a work of art. Nearby was the *msonge* of the late chief, his father,

built in the same way but dark and funereal inside. It contained his father's tomb, which was guarded by three old women who sat on the floor, statuesque in their immobility and maintaining absolute silence. I did not ask who they were. On the floor was the late chief's drum, a large instrument covered with dark red cow's hide. Hanging from a rail by papyrus cords were wooden milk jars, and in stalls at one side were young calves. Everything was preserved as in the old chief's lifetime, but no one was allowed to live in this *msonge* except the guardians of the tomb.

Another palace was that of Chief Alfred Kalemera of Kianja. It closely resembled a fortress, and was surrounded by two high circular walls with iron gates. Inside were two long stone houses. In one lived the Chief and his family, and in the other the women of the household and the domestic staff. Kalemera was nominally a Christian and so could not openly maintain a harem, but I had little doubt that some of the women in the second house had been concubines. Now they were mere status symbols, because the chief was a man of over sixty, enfeebled by disease, unable to walk without help and of little interest to any woman. His was a residence designed for defence against enemies, which did not surprise me because my researches into his past had shown that he was really a usurper and that the rightful chief was in exile.

On the day of my first call he was having his mid-day meal. It consisted of soup and a huge plate of meat and potatoes. After the meal an attendant brought him a basin of water and he washed his mouth and hands. The ritual was formal. The servants on duty behaved as if they were waiting upon a great potentate. It was impossible to ignore their look of abject subservience, as if fear of their master was the mainspring of their obedience to his commands.

Kalemera's forbears had had a reputation for cruelty which still survived in the memory of the people. His grandfather was reputed to be a lustful savage responsible for many executions. Perhaps Kalemera's servants believed that he could exercise similar powers at his whim, in spite of the British administration.

However, like his servants, Kalemera also lived in fear — of his enemies. Poison would be their likeliest weapon, so every dish and drink had to be tasted before being served to him. He was surrounded by a screen of witch doctors, the leader of whom was half-brother to a neighbouring sub-chief. This man enjoyed almost unlimited power and was virtual ruler of the Kianja chiefdom. Kalemera never took any decision without consulting him. He knew two words of English which he addressed to me as I left: they were 'Goodbye, sir'.

Chief Lweikiza of Bugabo had the smallest territory of all, but he too lived in a residence befitting the dignity of his position. The purpose of my visit to him in May 1942 was to adjudicate a boundary dispute between him and Chief Gabriel of Kiamtwara. The land involved was an abandoned European estate which, strictly, was Government property, but the Government had forgotten its existence and now both chiefs were fighting for its possession. I decided to frame my judgment on a precedent set by King Solomon. I suggested to Gabriel that he divide the land into two portions and give Lweikiza first choice of the divisions. The suggestion was declined, and I therefore had to make the decision. It pleased neither of them. On my return to Bukoba, Chief Lweikiza followed me and said that he had not slept a wink since my decision. The reply I gave him was not calculated to cure his insomnia.

It was while I was at Rubafu that Lweikiza, chatting with me one day, gave me some interesting information about the Germans' attitude towards some of the Bukoba chiefs at the outbreak of the 1914-18 War. The Germans suspected some of the chiefs of conspiring with the British in Uganda. Lweikiza was not chief at the time, but uncle of the reigning chief, Rugachwa, who bore him no goodwill. Rugachwa accused him of saying that he hoped the British would soon occupy the country, and Lweikiza was arrested. At about the same time Ntare, Chief of Karagwe, was charged with corresponding with the Uganda Government and, after only a few hours' investigation, was hanged along with his uncle and chief clerk.

After three days of acute mental agony Lweikiza was released. He described to me vividly how he stood under guard before the German commissioner on the third morning. The latter stroked his chin and pondered for an interminable time whether he would hang Lweikiza or not. Eventually he decided to let him go. 'I came out of the grave,' Lweikiza said to me. Evidently the German commissioners had power of life and death over the people in their Districts, at least in time of war. I assured Lweikiza that such a system would never have been tolerated in any Territory under British administration. I pointed out to him that the first principle of British law was the assumption that an accused person was innocent until his guilt was proved beyond doubt; and that to execute a man after a summary trial was abhorrent to our ideas of justice.

It was at Rubafu some months later that I again made contact with my African colleague of Bugufi days, Mapera bin Kyaruze. He hobbled several miles on crutches to my camp to see me. From Bugufi, he told me, he had gone to Kasulu as adviser to the chiefs of Uha and there in 1934 had lost a leg through snake-bite. Seriously handicapped in his work by this mishap, he had been retired without pension or gratuity — to the immense discredit of our Government.

Their excuse, I believe, was that responsibility for his case lay with the various Native Authorities he had served. I looked on this as a shabby subterfuge; was it not on Government orders that he had served these different authorities? As if this were not enough, an over-zealous Assistant District Officer had visited his village in 1938 and threatened to sell him up because he had not paid tax since the loss of his leg. I was sorry to think that we could mete out such treatment to so distinguished an African. This man had occupied positions of distinction and responsibility throughout his active life: in German times he had been appointed adviser to the young King Msinga of Ruanda, reputedly the most powerful chief in Africa, and this post had been tantamount to the governorship of the huge province of Ruanda. When we succeeded the Germans, the same man served us as adviser to some of the less experienced chiefs under our system of Indirect Rule. Now, because he was crippled, he had been thrown on the scrap-heap and treated as a common tax defaulter. Yet there was no bitterness in his talk to me. I gave him at once a certificate of permanent exemption from tax, and, although after much writing and representation of his case I failed to secure him a pension, I did succeed in persuading the Government to grant him a gratuity of 700 shillings.

The chiefs of Bukoba had not only a unified Native Treasury but also a chiefs' council. This was a deliberative assembly which met at the end of every month to discuss affairs of common interest, including treasury finances, and make recommendations to the District Commissioner. These recommendations, if approved, could be given the force of law under the Native Authority Ordinance. The Council had no administrative authority over the individual chiefs; its purpose was to encourage co-operation among them and promote a common policy whenever possible. But it had judicial functions of a civil nature, in which context it was the supreme Native Court, functioning both as a court of first instance and as a court of appeal from the judgments of the chiefs' courts. Appeals from its decisions lay to the District Commissioner and thence to the Provincial Commissioner at Mwanza. On the civil side, therefore, the Africans of Bukoba had ample opportunities of having their cases fully heard.

The District Commissioner did not attend the meetings of the chiefs' council except by invitation, or if he had some important communication to make. I had one trying session with it when I had to give reasons for the fall in coffee prices and explain the mysteries of the international market with its obedience to the law of supply and demand.

When I arrived in Bukoba, Lake arranged that I should take over

supervision of one group of chiefdoms, while he looked after the rest.
As a first-class magistrate, I also handled the serious court work.
This meant much extra toil, but I was glad to undertake it and our
arrangement worked well all the time Lake was in charge of the
District. To share our burdens were my old colleague from Ulanga,
Peter Bleakley, now an Assistant District Officer, and a junior
A.D.O. Lake also left to me most of the liaison work with the chiefs'
council and the supervision of the Native Treasury. This latter duty
I enjoyed most of all, and I gave what spare time I had to lecturing
the Native Authority clerks on the approved methods of keeping
their cash books and registers. To make the lectures intelligible
I borrowed a blackboard from the police superintendent.

This liaison work brought me into close touch with the African
secretary of the council, a Muhaya named Luamgira. His salary
was £600 a year, then a respectable sum, but he earned every penny
of it. His job was to keep the minutes of the council's deliberations
and the records of its judicial decisions; he was also responsible for
giving effect to the latter. He kept all council debates within the
bounds of reason and the law. Luamgira had been a loyal servant of
the former German Government and had fought for them in the
East African campaign of 1914-18. As a youth he had spent three
years at college in Berlin, and he spoke fluent German. For some
years after the war, out of loyalty to his former masters, he refused
employment under our Government. Eventually he was persuaded
to take the secretaryship of the newly-formed chiefs' council, after it
had been explained to him that in this capacity he would be serving
his tribe and not the British Government.

In my liaison work I had much to discuss with him, and I always
admired his frankness. He could be caustic about our relationship
with the chiefs; he thought we gave them too much power and
not enough discipline. This point of view was typical of the German
administrators with whom he had formerly worked. I pointed out
that if our system of Indirect Rule was to function properly we must
support the prestige and authority of every chief and not apply too
many brakes. He was never impressed by this argument, and I do
not think that he had much belief in Indirect Rule: as an educated
African he regarded the chiefs as a reactionary group hostile to
change, and favoured a more radical approach to the problems of
his country. In many aspects of my political work his advice and
help were invaluable; he was aware of every straw in the wind and
never failed to tell me of it.

In my early days at Bukoba I had the urge to revisit my old
district of Ngara, and Lake gave me leave to make the trip. It was
fifteen years since I had travelled the road through Biharamulo

and Keza to the Ruvuvu river. Of the two chiefs I had known, Nkundabagore of Usubi was dead. I visited his grave at Keza. It was like a mausoleum, the tomb being enclosed in a large chamber of burnt brick on high ground overlooking the country of Usubi — a fitting resting-place for its chief. The road down the escarpment to the Ruvuvu ferry was exactly as I had built it years before; but on the river my six-canoe pontoon had disappeared and been replaced by a contraption mounted on oil drums. Whereas my pontoon could carry a loaded lorry or two motor cars this one had capacity for only one car or an unloaded lorry. I happened to be travelling in a lorry carrying half a ton of lime for Ngara. Lorry and lime had to cross separately, and it took more than an hour to get everything over to the Ngara bank.

I found Chief Kinyamazinge greatly changed. Never intellectually strong, his mind had deteriorated with time, and now he had been retired in favour of his son. As the boy was still a minor and studying at the School for the Sons of Chiefs (a new foundation) at Tabora, the country of Bugufi was being administered by a council of regents. The Chief resented his retirement, and this figured prominently in our talk. His conversation was disconnected, and he tired of a subject almost as soon as he had opened it, but running through his disjointed remarks was the complaint that he had been badly treated. I could see that he had difficulty in remembering who I was, and after I had expressed my sympathy for his present condition, I took my leave.

At Ngara I was agreeably surprised to meet John Curry, the agricultural officer for the region, whose responsibilities covered the District of Bukoba, Biharamulo and Ngara. He had just returned from a visit to the Belgian Congo, and I had the satisfaction of telling him that he had used the road Mapera and I had built fifteen years before. I also showed him the administrative offices I had erected, and later we were entertained to a meal by the District Commissioner in the residence which I had begun but not completed. The mud hut in which I had lived was no longer there.

John drove me back to Bukoba, and on the way told me this story. The Belgian governor of a province which he visited had taken one of his D.C.s in his car for a road inspection. About 10 miles out they came to a cross-roads which lacked signposts. When the D.C. could give no good reason for their absence, he was made to leave the car and walk all the way back.

John had an appointment to meet this governor, who excused himself when the day arrived on the ground that he had to attend a public execution. In the Congo, it appeared, all executions were carried out in public, perhaps to convince the populace that when a man was condemned to death he was well and truly hanged. In Tanganyika all executions were performed inside the prison walls; representatives of the chief were invited to see the prisoner before execution and his body afterwards, but they were never allowed to see the actual execution. All death sentences were confirmed or commuted by the Governor after considering the reports of the trial judge and the District Commissioner of the condemned man's district. In the Congo death sentences had to be approved by the central government in Brussels.

As in all districts of the Territory, the basic economy of the Haya tribe was agricultural. The major crop was coffee. A recent census had given a return of 12 million trees, but there were probably more. They represented an average annual income of £300,000 at the then prevailing price of £30 a ton. It was now wartime and coffee had dropped in price. Nevertheless we reckoned that the individual grower could still achieve a cash yield of five times the amount of tax he had to pay.

The method of cultivation was to grow bananas between the rows of coffee trees and use the decaying banana leaves as mulch. A strong stock of cattle would have improved the soil: but between 1920 and 1940 the cattle population had been reduced by outbreaks of rinderpest from 400,000 to 50,000 head. This was a heavy blow to the Haya economy, both as regards milk supply and manure. Even so, the output of coffee and other crops could, have been greatly increased but for the indolence of the men, who left most of the work to the women. Secretary Luamgira was alive to this, and had organised the Haya Agricultural Association to encourage the men to abandon their lazy habits and do their share of cultivation. Its membership was not large, but he worked with quiet persistence to increase it. I gave him every possible support.

John Curry saw with dismay the lack of cleaning in the coffee *shambas*. The chiefs were also concerned about this, and made regulations under the Native Authority Ordinance prescribing fines for *shamba* neglect. The Native Court registers teemed with coffee cases, and the fines imposed achieved some purpose, but Curry yearned for the methods employed against indolent coffee growers in the Belgian Congo. There a village headman could whip the owner of a dirty *shamba*, and Curry remarked to me how spotlessly clean the Congolese *shambas* were. Such a procedure could never have been permitted by our Government, and I doubted its long-term efficacy. A coffee industry promoted under the sting of the whip would have had a precarious existence.

The coffee regulations for Tanganyika provided that our pur-chasers of coffee for re-sale must hold a licence from the District

Commissioner. In Bukoba the licences were held by five or six Indian merchants. They were resentful of newcomers to the trade, and when a rich Indian with many trading interests in the Territory purchased the local coffee-curing factory and introduced a policy of increased prices to encourage increased production, they tried to form a ring against him. These rings caused much discontent among the growers. There was also illegal buying by unlicensed Arabs and others, and our courts were kept busy punishing these offenders. By late 1942, the position had become so confused and unsatisfactory that the Government appointed a coffee board for the District with powers to control all buying and marketing of the crop. This put an end to the rings and protected the Haya from exploitation by unscrupulous middlemen.

The first secretary of this board was one of a colony of Jewish refugees whom, midway through the war, the London Government decided to move from Cyprus to parts of British Africa. A number of these came to Bukoba, and their housing and maintenance became another of our wartime duties. We managed to find them accommodation in some former German buildings outside the town, and there they remained until the end of the war. Among them was a distinguished Berlin throat specialist, who joined our hospital staff as an honorary consultant and performed some operations during his stay. All these Jews were penniless, having been stripped of their property as the price of escaping from Hitler's Germany. With the exception of one or two difficult individuals, they contributed in no small way to the social life of the community.

Another factor that prejudiced the improvement of coffee production was the introduction of military conscription. In 1942 a Government ordinance subjected Africans to conscription 'for the defence of the Territory'. It proved a popular measure, because service in the Army meant good pay and exemption from the unpopular task of *shamba* cultivation. The smartness and fit condition of men returning on leave encouraged others to join up for what was obviously the good life. However, as I believed it was essential to balance the needs of the armed forces with the requirements of agriculture, I set up an unofficial tribunal to inquire into all doubtful cases and caused it to be widely known that aggrieved parties could appeal to me against the call-up of their sons. I did this with Lake's approval and at the behest of the Agricultural Department. The tribunal fully justified its existence. Since the conscription law had to be applied through the Native Authorities, there was ample opportunity for village headmen, sub-chiefs and even chiefs to pay off old scores against people they disliked. My tribunal brought this to light, and quite a few conscripted boys were returned to their homes. A typical case was that of a father who had been conscripted along with his son, leaving the mother alone to look after the *shamba*. I released them both. It was my policy to see that at least one son remained with the father on the *shamba*. If the father were dead, then two sons at least had to stay at home.

It was possible to enforce these tribunal decisions because recruits remained at least three months in Bukoba before being despatched to a central depot. A camp outside the town was established to accommodate them. If this had not been done there would have been very few recruits. The average standard of physical fitness was so low that we had to build up the stamina of every man before we dared submit him for medical examination. Many suffered from malnutrition, a consequence of their indolent way of life. But not all their ailments were from this cause. The assistant district officer who had charge of the camp told me that over 40 per cent of the recruits required treatment for venereal disease.

The maintenance of the camp not only meant a reduction of agricultural manpower but was a drain on our existing food supplies. Our stocks were so low at one time that I persuaded the Provincial Commissioner in April 1943 to suspend recruitment. Unfortunately this suspension did not last long; the bureaucrats were soon on our backs, and recruiting was resumed by order in June. In July the food position had again become critical, and we had to obtain leave to import 200 tons of rice and cassava. Thieving from *shambas* spread widely, and the prison was crammed with robbers.

In September 1942 John Curry left us on transfer to the Bahamas and was replaced by an old friend of Korogwe days, Frederick Thomas. It was nine years since we had worked together, and I welcomed his arrival. In November news came to me on safari that Frederick Lake was ill with pneumonia, and I was ordered to return at once and assume charge of the District. After a long and dangerous illness, he eventually made a good recovery but had to go on sick leave and, to my regret, did not return to Bukoba.

My first concern on taking over the District was to work with Thomas on a food-production campaign. The human material at our disposal made it a difficult task. The Government wanted 2,000 tons of maize from Bukoba and as many groundnuts as possible. Maize planting was to be the subject of a compulsory order, but before beginning the campaign we carried out an experiment at Minziro in the chiefdom of Bugabo to see how long it would take one person to prepare an acre for planting. Our test showed that the average male could complete the task in twenty-seven days — not bad for a Muhaya. We allowed another six days for two weedings and two days for sundries, and calculated that thirty-five days in all were needed to produce a reasonable crop.

The campaign was not a success, as only 300 tons of maize were grown. The chiefs blamed recruiting and wayward rains for the shortfall. These had certainly contributed to it, but an important additional cause was human fallibility. It seemed to me strange to blame the rains for crop failures in a country so generously watered. There were abundant streams that could have been used for irrigation by an industrious people, but as always we were up against social customs that put a premium on male sloth. It was Bugufi over again.

About this time I came across a German surveyor who had been paroled. He told me that he had been sent to Bukoba in 1913 to explore the possibility of an irrigation scheme based on the waters of the Kagera. He was confident that if there had been no war in 1914 the Germans would have harnessed this great river and put millions of acres under cultivation. This could well have been so, but I could not help harbouring the thought that so monumental a scheme would have been devised for European rather than African benefit and that there would have been great European estates where now the Bahaya were growing their coffee.

The inducement to grow groundnuts was monetary, and in this connection I experienced a sample of bureaucratic lack of scruple. Groundnuts were needed for our armies in Egypt, and the Government had promised a minimum price of ten cents a pound to every grower. The promise was announced in the *Official Gazette*. The crop was to be purchased at not less than this price by selected merchants, and the Government was to make good any loss of profit they might suffer. The prospect of cash always appealed to the Bahaya, and several hundred acres of groundnuts were planted, although I suspected that the women did most of the work. When the crop was due for picking a telegram came from the Treasury intimating that the Government did not wish to stand by its guarantee in view of the loss involved, and requesting District Commissioners to persuade the people to accept a lower price. I told the Provincial Commissoner that I could not comply with this request and make myself a party to a flagrant breach of faith. He sympathised, especially as he had received similar responses from other D.C.s. Eventually the Government was obliged to honour its undertaking. One point I made at the time was that failure to implement a solemn promise of this nature would make a welcome item of news for German propaganda.

During the controversy all D.C.s. received a confidential letter from the Treasury which took the prize for cynicism. The writer suggested that in Districts where the groundnut growers were restive and antagonistic to the suggestion of a price reduction it should be shelved, but that in Districts where growers were indifferent or less sophisticated a reduced price could safely be applied. This letter was completely ignored.

Bukoba had a wolfram mine and some tin deposits. With Malaya closed to the Allies as a source of supply of these minerals, our local mines assumed some importance. The wolfram mine, from which steel-hardening tungsten is derived, was located at Kibanda in the Karagwe chiefdom. This mine had been taken over by the Government and was being operated by two South African miners.

The occasion of my first visit there was to investigate the shooting of an African worker by one of these men. I found manslaughter against him, but had to realise that the place was as much to blame for the crime as the man himself. I have rarely visited a more God-forsaken spot. It had to be approached in a rickety dugout canoe over a swift-flowing river and then by eight miles of walking through tsetse-infested bush. The Europeans lived in mud huts on a bare hillside with nothing around but sand and rock. There were 500 African workers. Drinking water had to be fetched from several miles away, except during the rains when the run-off from the hut roofs could be collected in drums. The local water was only to be found in stagnant ponds, but was so filthy that I could neither wash nor shave for the three days I spent there.

I found the two South Africans highly nervous, and the African labour in a mood of rebellion, resenting their virtual incarceration in this unwholesome place. The dead African had been drunk and had adopted a threatening attitude with spear and club. The European seized his rifle, whereupon the African ran amok through the camp. The European's nerves, already taut from days or weeks of tension, snapped, and he fired the fatal shot. I gave him bail pending the decision of the Government's law officers on the case, and allowed him to stay with his companion, who was in too nervous a state to be left alone. I admonished the labour force before I left, and warned them to stay sober.

Before Frederick Lake's illness, and with his full agreement, I had been investigating the affairs and record of Chief Alfred Kalemera, noted throughout the Territory as one of the most highly paid chiefs. It had always been my view—which was shared by most administrative officers—that the African tribesman was entitled to the best government that Indirect Rule could provide and should be spared the rule of corrupt or ineffective chiefs. If we allowed such men to stay in power we were consciously betraying our trust. Indirect Rule was not only designed to restore the ancient rights and laws of the tribes but also to bring benefits to their peoples, and this could not be achieved if we failed to provide reliable and competent leaders. Chief Kalemera did not in the least comply with the required standards. He was old, physically crippled by disease and a prey to fears of witchcraft. He took no active part in the administration of his country and the witch-doctors who screened him from danger and his sub-chiefs did more or less what they liked. One sub-chief was gaoled for manufacturing a very dangerous type of illicit liquor. In spite of his high salary Kalemera was heavily in debt to Indian merchants—a state of affairs that opened up possible avenues of corruption—and it was significant that there was more illegal coffee-buying in his country than anywhere else. The Chief was unpopular with the mass of his people and with the influential elders, for the very good reason that by the law of the royal Batinda clan he was a usurper.

Kalemera's accession came about in this way. The former Chief, Kahigi, was growing old and as he still had no sons and feared that he might die without having named a successor, he nominated Kalemera, his next of kin at the time. So Kalemera was very much of a Hobson's choice. Then shortly before the old chief died his favourite Batinda spouse bore a son to whom he gave the name Mutembei, and Kahigi decided to change his political testament and nominate the boy as his successor. He declared this intention to the elders, but death overtook him before his decision could be put in writing for submission to Government. The Kalemera faction ousted the infant chief and his supporters, suppressed all evidence of Mutembei's nomination, and persuaded the Government to accept Kalemera as the rightful chief. All this had happened in 1921, and for almost twenty-two years the British administration had maintained a usurper as chief in Kianja to the great disadvantage of the people. Mutembei, for his safety, had gone to live in exile at Dar-es-Salaam, where he had a job in a Government department.

In Kianja uneasy lay the head of Kalemera, who feared witchcraft or other forms of malevolence from his enemies, and the affairs of the tribe deteriorated through lack of proper administration. This deterioration had to be halted, if possible by the chief's deposition.

It is never easy to have a chief deposed and this was particularly true in the case of Kalemera. The District records showed that for ten years D.C.s had been trying to bring about his removal, but without success. The Secretariat preferred to let sleeping dogs lie. I was now seeking not only to have the Chief removed but his sub-chiefs also—in other words, the entire upper structure of the Native Authority. I therefore had to make out a good case. My memorandum on the subject was submitted to the Government in December 1942. To soften the blow I recommended that the chief be retired on health grounds. I had to wait four months for a reply, but in April 1943 the Governor himself signified his approval of my proposals and decreed that the chief be retired on pension.

On 18 May the Provincial Commissioner arrived from Mwanza to deliver the Governor's verdict. The interview was not pleasant. Kalemera refused to retire voluntarily. We then told him that he would be forcibly retired on pension and given a house in Bukoba to reside in. The next day I left for Kianja to organise a full meeting of the Batinda clan and the tribe in general to elect a new Chief. The actual selection would be made by the Batinda, but it was necessary for the tribe to be represented at this assembly. Meanwhile a full police guard was put on the Chief's palace. On 20 May 1943 7,000 people assembled at Kanazi, the Chief's village. Chairs for the administrative staff were placed in front of the courthouse. Facing us was the roped enclosure for the members of the Batinda clan and the sub-chiefs; behind them were the elders of the tribe, and behind them again were the ordinary villagers. The election of Mutembei was almost unanimous and the Provincial Commissioner formally accepted him as Chief on behalf of the Government. The excitement was tremendous, and the huge crowd broke into a storm of cheering.

My next task was to send to Bukoba all Kalemera's personal effects, plus a milch cow. For this purpose I had to visit the palace. In the ex-Chief's own residence, behind a bundle of tent canvases, I found a picture turned to the wall. It was a portrait of the ex-Kaiser, Wilhelm II. Kalemera would have been a young man of thirty when the Germans left Bukoba. Had he kept this portrait as a memento, or as an insurance against their possible return?

Kalemera was determined to make things as difficult as possible for his successor. His first move was to obtain the Provincial Commissioner's consent to the removal of the corrugated iron roof from his own quarters in the palace. Backed by the Batinda elders I vetoed this, pointing out that it was a fixture and, therefore, the property of the reigning Chief. I also observed that since the Government were giving Kalemera the free gift of a house, he could not possibly want this roofing for his own use. Presumably he intended to sell the corrugated iron to one of his Indian creditors as part payment for a debt.

Mutembei arrived in mid-June and was given a great welcome by his people. We tried to keep the date of his coming secret, but this proved impossible, and on the day that the steamer carrying him berthed at Bukoba pier, the approaches to the harbour were thronged with thousands of Kianja tribesmen who had come to greet the long-exiled chief. Mutembei soon settled into his chiefdom. Luamgira was a good friend to him, and I was always at hand if he needed advice or help. I was more anxious than most that he should rule his country well and promote the prosperity of his people. He frequently consulted me and we worked closely together while I was in Bukoba. After leaving the District I lost touch and never heard how he fared afterwards.

The deposition of Kalemera had a salutary effect on the other chiefs. They learned the lesson that no chief's position was impregnable and that if he were indifferent to his duty, he could be overthrown. As intrigue was rife in many 'royal' families, and there were relatives always ready to campaign against a chief if things went wrong, the Kalemera incident encouraged most chiefs to take an increased interest in administration.

One sequel to the affair was a visit paid to me at midnight by Chief Gabriel of Kiatwara. I was asleep, and awoke to find him at my bedside. My immediate reaction was to think that something was gravely wrong, but it turned out that he had come to express to me his fears that a half-brother and a cousin were intriguing against his position. One of his policemen had misbehaved, and they were seeking to implicate him in the man's misconduct. I knew about this case and assured the Chief that I would not listen to intrigues against him. If people had accusations to make, they could do so in open court.

The crime rate in Bukoba was higher than anything I had known elsewhere. The average level of African wealth per head was higher there than in most other parts of the Territory. The predominant crimes were larceny, burglary and robbery with violence. I must have tried some hundreds of cases during my term of service. Adult criminals were incarcerated in the local prison; youthful offenders were sent to a reformatory at Tabora, which had been opened in 1939. Previously youths had been caned rather than exposed to association with hardened criminals in prison, but caning had not proved very successful, and more often than not the delinquents had continued in their careers of crime. The indolence of the Haya villager, his dislike of work in the fields and the lure of the towns and trading settlements were causes of the crime wave.

Shortly before the time of which 1 write a tablet had come on the market which was reputed to cure gonorrhea. It was known as M. & B. 693. As a good percentage of Bukoba males suffered from this complaint and had an almost religious faith in the tablet, the demand for it was constant and considerable. There were wholesale thefts of it from hospitals and dispensaries, and illegal sales from the

same sources by the African staffs, who thus made handsome addi-
tions to their wages. Large consignments of the drug were also stolen
in transit by railway and customs employees. The work of our courts
was increased by cases involving these malpractices. There were also
cases of African quacks travelling round the district with hypodermic
syringes and stolen medicines offering instant cures for venereal
disease.

A supposed sovereign remedy for syphilis was an injection of
bismuth, which cost 2 shillings. At least one patient was known to
have died from this treatment, and others became dangerously ill.
It was these outbreaks of illness that led to some of the offenders
being caught, but many must have pursued their anti-social calling
undiscovered.

The Government's police were too few to cope with all this crime,
and there was urgent need for a Native Authority police force, but
the Chiefs' treasury was not strong enough financially to bear this
expense. Every chief had a small private police squad, mainly for
his personal protection and paid from his private purse, but these
had no relevance to the prevention of crime. It would have needed
many years, thousands more tons of production and much greater
tax yields before the chiefs' council could have organised a comprehensive system of crime prevention.

Murder too was prevalent. During my tour at least a dozen
murderers were executed in Bukoba gaol. Highway robbery and
private vengeance were two common motives. I tried one case under
extended jurisdiction in which a Mrundi named Ndabahalanye
from my old district of Ngara was charged with assisting three others
to carry out a vendetta killing. Ndabahalanye held the victim's legs
while the others depatched him: for this he was rewarded with a
payment of 30 shillings. I learned after the trial that he was the local
witch-doctor: he was convicted and subsequently hanged. The actual
killers, who were tried by the Chief Justice of the Territory, were
acquitted for lack of evidence. Such are the intricacies of the
criminal law.

A case of highway robbery on the Bukoba-Ngara border involving
four Warundi tribesmen resulted in their conviction and execution
in September 1943. In this case also one of the murderers was a
witch-doctor. He carried a bunch of sisal leaves which he brandished
in the faces of the intended victims with the intention of paralysing
their powers of resistance. I visited these four men in prison a few
days before their execution. They looked far fitter than when they
had been arrested, and had all put on weight. The minds of these
men were mercifully curtained against visions of the future, and

they had no realisation of their approaching fate. Only at the very last moment did they appreciate that something unpleasant was going to happen to them.

In the cases I have described witchcraft figured as an ancillary to the act of murder. However, in most cases witchcraft or the fear of it was the main motive of the crime, and in all these cases the murderous act took the form of hut-burning. So widespread did hut-burning become that the Chiefs' council, at our instance, passed a law compelling the people of a village where a hut had been burnt to rebuild it without payment.

The motive of this type of murder was based on the African belief that any person, particularly a child, who died before completing the normal span of life was the victim of witchcraft. The parents of the deceased child or the relatives of the deceased husband or wife quietly conducted the search for the warlock and, when he and his family were asleep, and generally during a dry period when grass would burn readily, would set fire to his hut. Because the thatched roof and wooden components were highly combustible, an entire family could be trapped and consumed by the flames before they could be aware of what was happening. Escapes from this death were very rare, and usually the warlock's entire family succumbed. Holocausts of this kind did not shock the other villagers. Being believers in witchcraft themselves, they took the view that, if the principal victim were a warlock, it was no cause for regret that his wife and children were also done to death, because they too could be potential witches. Better to destroy the whole brood than the parent snake alone.

Many of these murderers freely confessed to their action: they thought it no crime to destroy those who had already killed members of their own families. As it was part of my duty to submit a report to the Governor on all condemned persons, I had a busy time writing reports. I had mixed feelings about the hanging of these people, but the Governor had no doubts—and no reprieve was ever granted to the perpetrator of a hut-burning murder.

Frederick Lake, with whom I frequently discussed this harrassing problem, ascribed the prevalence of witchcraft murders to the inadequacy of the medical services supplied by the Government. If all those whose deaths led to these murders could have received skilled treatment they would probably have recovered and there would have been no murders.

There was one other class of murder that should be mentioned —that of the unfaithful wife by her returning soldier husband. There was a general belief among Bahaya who joined the army that the King's uniform conferred immunity against the ordinary processes of law, and that a soldier who killed the wife who had betrayed him would be safe from punishment thanks to the protection of King George.

Samuel, a baptized member of one of the missions, was a soldier who nourished this belief. Returning on leave he found that his wife had been living with another man while he was on active service. He killed her. In court before me he declared that the King, whose soldier he was, would protect him from harm. My duty was to commit him for trial. He was convicted and hanged. Any clemency towards crimes of this kind would have put many soldiers' wives in danger, because fidelity to absent husbands was not widely practised.

A sub-chief, distressed that his sexual powers were waning, applied to an old woman famed for her magical powers for a brew to restore his manhood. When the medicine did not immediately prove effective, he savagely assaulted her, believing that what she had compounded was really intended to aggravate his condition. When, later, it apparently proved effective the sub-chief proudly demonstrated his restored powers with four buxom wenches in his own hut in the presence of the village elders.

My journal records that on 9 October 1943 a deputation of women from the country of the Bugabo asked me to depose Chief Lweikiza because he had failed to bring rain. They were deadly serious, and this was the first inkling I had that Lweikiza was credited with magical powers. In reply I asked them if I should also depose the other Bukoba chiefs, since the shortage of rain was widespread. The question nonplussed them, but I carefully avoided giving the impression that I did not share their belief in the Chief's rain-making ability. I expressed sympathy with their troubles and voiced the hope that rain would soon come.

Among the Haya there was a rigid caste system that defined the relationship between the chiefs and their subjects. All chiefs belonged to the royal Batinda clan, into which no commoner could marry. Only children born of a Batinda mother were eligible for succession to the chieftainship, unless there were none living. In that event the reigning chief had to select an heir from the offspring of his concubines. Kalemera, for example, was born of a non-Batinda mother.

The women were the beasts of burden. They did all the tilling of land and growing of food. The only manual labour undertaken by the men was the cleaning of the coffee and banana plantations, but even this was often passed on to immigrant Africans from Belgian Ruanda who came in search of food.

A woman could not inherit land on intestacy. On the contrary, she and her children were inherited by her husband's heirs. If there were no heirs or next of kin the chief took over the inheritance. If property were left to a woman by will, the relatives of the deceased testator had to approve the will before it could take effect. The relatives who inherited the widow were only obliged to supply her with food and shelter. If she rejected their maintenance her one recourse was to return to her father's house, but if she did that, she had to leave her children behind.

To elope with a girl without her father's consent was punishable, under our dispensation, with a fine or imprisonment. The man concerned was also liable to pay the amount of the dowry to the outraged parent, but sometimes payment of the dowry sufficed to mollify him and led to sanctioning of the marriage. The result was very different if the man were a commoner and the girl a Batinda. Since no marriage was possible and the chief's dignity had been seriously offended, the punishment would be a heavy fine or imprisonment. In pre-European days the offender would probably have had to pay with his life.

The single girl had no say in her future. Before marriage she was the property of her family, and after marriage that of her husband. If her lover could not marry her she became damaged goods: no longer a virgin and still unmarried, her value for dowry was low. Her family would be glad to get rid of her at any cost.

There was a government ordinance which imposed severe penalties for intercourse with girls under the age of consent, which was fixed at twelve years. This law should have been invoked in all such cases, but the Bahaya did not consider the offence any more serious than elopement, and it is not always prudent to give effect to European laws in an African community if its own laws take a more lenient view of the act in question. A case came before me for review of a youth who had been fined 10 shillings—for him this was a large sum—for having connection with a girl of nine years. I could have withdrawn the case to my own court where the offender would have received a substantial term of imprisonment, but the girl's family had been suitably recompensed and did not wish the case to go further. Therefore I took no further action; and besides, the girl had consented fully to the act of seduction, and could possibly have been the more active of the two participants.

One of the most important laws affecting females was the strange on. of *bisisi*. Under this, the man who had sexual intercourse with a woman was presumed to be the father of her next child. For example, A., an unmarried woman, sleeps with B., her lover. Some months later she marries C., and a year later bears a child. B., by the *bisisi* law, is deemed to be the father of that child and can claim it. However, any later children that A. may have while married to C. will belong to C. If C. divorces her and she marries D., the first child of her marriage to D. can be claimed by C.

This custom suggests that no period of gestation was recognised by the Bahaya. It gave rise to countless cases in the Native Courts and appeals to me. No doubt the appellants hoped that I would override their tribal law, but this I neither could nor would do.

One of our most important chiefs, who shall be nameless, was a *bisisi* child. His true father had discarded his mother, who had married again and given birth to a boy, whom the *bisisi* father immediately claimed and nominated as his successor. The child bore not the slightest resemblance to his reputed father. If the people had only known it, they had, biologically speaking, a non-royal child on the throne.

In all customs relating to marriage among tribal peoples the dowry was, and still is, the basic principle. No dowry, no marriage. Dowry was paid in the prevailing tribal currency: in Bukoba it was cattle. The normal rate, paid to the bride's father, was one cow. Where the bride had some exceptional qualities, more than one might be demanded.

The criterion of female beauty among the Bahaya was buxomness. Fat was beautiful. Skinny women were regarded with disfavour, although in some parts of the District a woman with a long neck would have claims to beauty.

The husband could divorce his wife at any time and claim back the dowry, but some of our more progressive chiefs had amended this law by ruling that if there were children of the marriage the amount of dowry returnable must be reduced. At Maruku in Chief Daudi Rugomora's court it was ruled that where the dowry cow had calved and the girl had already borne her husband a son the calf or calves would stay with the girl's father and only the cow be returned to the divorcing husband. I was glad to congratulate the chief on this enlightened judgement.

For ten months after her first marriage a bride could not raise her voice, or show her face in the company of men other than her husband. One such bride came with a case to me and spoke through her husband's sister, the husband being away in the army. All through the hearing she kept her head averted and never looked in my direction.

To marry a girl who was already betrothed to another was taboo. On one occasion a man guilty of this was fined 25 shillings. Unable to pay, and threatened with the sale of his *shamba*, he appealed to me to be allowed to expiate the offence by a term of imprisonment. With the chief's consent I gave him two months, and he was loud in his expressions of gratitude.

Women were debarred from milking in the belief that a cow milked by a woman would go dry. I never could fathom the logic of this custom. Women were used for the cultivation of food because they were the symbols of fertility; seed had to be planted by females if it were to germinate. Women also supplied milk to nourish their infants, often suckling them up to the age of two. On this analogy the milking of cows by women should have prolonged their milk flow rather than curtailing it.

A woman could not sue her husband for divorce except on the ground that he was impotent. There were quite a number of cases of this kind in the Native Courts. I often suspected that many of the claims were spurious, since women could not obtain release from marriage on any other ground. Tribal law gave few rights to women, but at least it recognised the right to a full married life.

No account of Haya custom would be complete without mention of the concubines known as *wajakazi* (singular, *mjakazi*). Concubinage was beginning to decline in the face of missionary opposition and administrative disapproval, but there were still traces of it in my time.

The *wajakazi* were the female slaves of the chief. If he took a fancy to a pretty wench she was brought to his palace, and if she bore a child it was his. Chiefs often rewarded their *wajakazi* with grants of land. These were life tenancies, to which descendants of the grantees could succeed if they paid the customary rent. This custom came to light in a case which Chief Petro Mugunda of Ihangiro brought to me, claiming rent from one of his tenants. On previous occasions his claim had been disallowed, but when he produced a book containing the names of 900 tenants and signed by a D.C. of several years earlier, the claim had to be admitted. Some of these grants had been made by himself, but the great majority of them had been spread over many previous generations and represented grants made by his ancestors to their own *wajakazi*. The custom provided one of the few circumstances in which a female could hold land in her own right.

The Roman Catholic White Fathers, members of a well entrenched organisation, did not take kindly to some of these customs. Embarrassing incidents resulted in which they came off second-best. Wills made by Haya Christians leaving property to the mission or to Christian wives in defiance of tribal law had to be declared invalid, to the intense annoyance of certain priests. Marriages between Christian girls and pagan husbands, if conducted in accordance with tribal rites, also aroused their wrath. In one such case an African mission teacher seized the girl and brought her to mission premises whither she was followed by her parents and the irate husband. She had, of course, to be surrendered, but the missionaries, to avoid loss of face, handed her over to the sub-chief of the area, himself a Christian. I ordered him to release the girl to her parents and stay out of the affair.

In another case a boy and girl, both members of the mission at Marauku and very much in love, were being instructed in the meaning of Christian marriage. Impatient at the length of the course, they went off and got married under tribal law, which simply meant that the boy's father paid dowry to the girl's. The priest, hearing of this, assembled a crowd of his followers after mass one Sunday, and went with them to the young husband's house, where they discovered the bride hiding behind a bush. They dragged her off to the mission. Her father, trying to protect her, was badly beaten. In the resultant case before the chief's court five Africans, including the mission teacher of the locality, were sentenced to terms of imprisonment. I heard the appeal in a packed court, the majority of the public being mission members, who included some African priests and teachers. I dismissed the appeal, but I told the convicted men that they could appeal above me to the Provincial Commissioner. This suggestion they rejected. The affair had already received sufficient publicity.

One White Father was in the habit of beating his parishioners if they disobeyed his wishes. On one occasion, on his orders, a catechist slapped the face of a woman who had refused to increase her church offerings. The catechist was prosecuted and fined in a sub-chief's court. The priest then tried to pressurise the chief into quashing the conviction. The chief, to his credit, refused.

These were acts of over-zealous priests and their underlings; they were in no way approved by the heads of the mission, with whom we maintained friendly relations.

There was friction between the Bahaya and the White Fathers over land. In 1905 the German Government, in conformity with its policy of using the missions as allies in the field of administration, had given the White Fathers a free grant of 3,600 acres, allegedly for the purpose of creating a land barrier between the warring chiefs of Bugabo and Kiamtwara. In consequence the Haya cultivators of this region became tenants of the mission and liable to pay rent to their new landlords. With the passage of time and the growth of political consciousness, these tenants or their successors claimed that the obligation to pay rent was a denial of their traditional rights. Led by their chiefs, they agitated for the return of the land to the tribe. The mission heads were well aware that this agitation, if prolonged, would be bad for their Christian image. They applied to Rome for instructions, and, after much correspondence to and fro, were permitted to sell 1,500 acres to the Government. The money was to be provided by the Chiefs' Treasury and paid to the mission authorities when a survey of the area had been completed by a Government surveyor. The fact that the mission had received the land free in the first instance and had been receiving rent for it for close on forty years, and that the Bahaya were really purchasing their own land, was tactfully ignored. It was my task, in co-operation with the surveyor, to fix the boundaries of the area to be restored to the people. A large slice still remained in mission hands, but for the time being the land hunger of the Bahaya seemed to have been appeased.

The White Fathers won many converts, but perhaps the most important, if not the most beneficial, result of their work was its influence on the women. The lowly status of the female in this tribal society was in direct conflict with Christian teaching, and the women were not slow to derive encouragement from this. Many of the younger women had become mission followers and were in revolt against their conditions. Unfortunately their revolt took a social rather than a religious form, and expressed itself in a loosening of family ties and indulgence in prostitution. An expert on population and vital statistics who had been commissioned to investigate social conditions in Bukoba reported that the population was in decline owing to the laxity of the women and the ravages of venereal disease. He regarded these factors as complementary, and ascribed them to the low status of women in the social life of the community. Figures he produced revealed an infant mortality rate of 400 in 1,000 live births.— which was normal for East Africa generally. The medical officer agreed with the findings of this report, and said that nearly 40 per cent of the population was suffering from venereal disease in one form or another. This seemed a staggering estimate, but the man who made it was not given to exaggeration. It was the gradual erosion of tribal discipline over the years which led to increasing promiscuity among the younger generation of women, and the spread of disease. It is a fair conclusion that the impact of mission teaching on African custom was the catalyst of these unwelcome developments.

The war and the recruitment of African males contributed to the spread of prostitution. Nairobi in Kenya was packed with black troops, and a large proportion of the prostitutes who operated there came from Bukoba. Every ship sailing from Bukoba to Kisumu, on the Kenya shore of the lake, carried a load of Haya girls. Some were married women travelling with the knowledge and implied consent of their husbands.

Our social investigator blamed the chiefs for the breakdown in morals, maintaining that if women were given a higher status they would be better behaved and that their present immoral conduct was an escape from the conditions of virtual slavery in which they were held. In his view the chiefs were unwilling to take a lead in reforming the customs relating to women. This was not quite fair. Some chiefs were willing to introduce reforms and had tried to do so, but were confronted by the resistance of reactionary groups of elders who resented any change. It is never easy to introduce reforms into so conservative a society as that of an African tribe. They have to come gradually with the spread of education, growing economic wealth and contact with the cultures of more advanced peoples. Sudden change can do more harm than good.

In my view it was the impact of Roman Catholic moral theology on the tribal laws of the Bahaya that caused much of the social disruption. Undoubtedly the cure for the injustices of Haya law lay in improving the lot of the women and giving them greater security in marriage. The Catholic priests argued that this could be achieved by breaking down the oppressive laws. This attitude was both absurd and impossible: if the chiefs could not reform the laws, no one else could. The wiser course would have been to add laws that would make the going hard for the idle male; to compel the men to take their full share of the work would, I believed, create healthier social conditions; and this could be done under the powers conferred by law on the Native Authorities. This was the policy that Luamgira advocated. He believed, with me, that this was the way to restore the moral and physical welfare of the Haya tribe without damaging its social structure.

The Bahaya had a strange custom relating to the joint ownership of chattels. It was not uncommon for four or five persons to own one cow, but jointure of ownership was on a different principle from ours. The cow was divided physically into a number of shares. Thus one person had a hind leg, another a fore leg, another the right side, and so on. While the cow was alive its earnings were also shared. If a calf were born each shareholder had a corresponding part to that which he held in the mother. If the cow were in milk each shareholder drank the milk for a month in turn. When the cow died the various parts were given to their respective owners.

Tropical countries are not health resorts. For officers in our service, home leave every two and a half years was deemed essential to build up bodily resistance to tropical malaise. During the war all these rules were abandoned, and our tours were extended indefinitely. As they lengthened, the graph of sickness mounted. At

the same time administrative duties increased, occasioned both by
wartime requirements and by the secondment of administrative
personnel to the occupied Italian territories. The young men went
off to the new jobs with glamorous military rank and high pay
while the old hands stayed behind to do the extra work, but not
for extra pay.

In my second year at Bukoba the entire District staff worked at
least twelve hours a day. My own day was often longer, and there
was no let-up on Sundays. After twenty-one years of tropical
service the strain began to tell on me. In July 1943 I was down for
five days with fever, my fourth severe attack in six months. Throughout that year I had been off duty for a total of ninety days through
illness. This was neither good for myself nor for the service.
Eventually, in January 1944, I was sent before a medical board
and ordered on sick leave to South Africa. At Cape Town in March
another medical board advised me to retire. I accepted its advice
and my career in the Colonial Service came to an end.

13

FINALE

It has been the fashion to criticise unfavourably the manner in which Great Britain acquired certain of her colonial possessions. Such criticisms have no application to the Territory with which this book is concerned. Tanganyika was not obtained by conquest nor by aggressive action of any kind against its inhabitants. The British entered it as trustees of the League of Nations, and were responsible to that body for the good government of its inhabitants.

We have already stated the principle of the Mandate under which administration was assumed: to promote the welfare of the indigenous peoples. Should there be a conflict between their interests and those of other races the interests of the former were to be treated as paramount. This principle proved easier to enunciate than to implement. Entrenched interests are hard to dislodge, and money often speaks with power.

Our problem in applying the mandatory principle was twofold—political and economic. It was our declared intention to train the Tanganyika Africans for eventual self-government. This was indeed, a long-term policy because of the multitude of tribes in the Territory, each claiming independence of the rest. Nevertheless it was genuinely undertaken, and we believed that with the passage of time the tribes would learn to co-operate and work together for the good of all.

The operation of Indirect Rule had its faults and, of course, its critics. Instructions regarding the selection of Native Authorities were often carried out in the letter rather than in the spirit, and we found ourselves in several instances with small units that should never have been resurrected and had later to be merged into larger ones. Many of the newly selected chiefs, however, proved excellent administrators, and their prowess confirmed us in the belief that our policy was right. Admittedly we had revived the hereditary principle, which was condemned by the new progressive schools of political thought, but it was indigenous to African custom and we felt justified in encouraging it. If later generations of Africans required a change it was for them to work out the necessary reforms.

We visualised the time when, with a more progressive outlook coming from a new generation of educated chiefs, there would be widespread amalgamation of treasuries—at first within Districts and later within Provinces—to be followed by tribal co-operation in economic enterprises, such as road-building and irrigation schemes. If you pool your cash, you usually pool your ideas of spending it. From these beginnings would evolve larger combinations—councils of chiefs with enlarged powers, administering broader areas. We conceived the eventual establishment of a centrally placed African government co-ordinating the activities of these councils and so maintaining the framework of the indigenous tribal organisations within a wider unity.

Later events did not permit such a consummation. The outbreak of the Second World War, by which the Colonial Powers were exhausted, subsequently relinquishing their responsibilities, led to the achievement of independence by Tanganyika and other African countries. This meant the end of Indirect Rule. The college-educated African, who had absorbed European political ideas and was now in control of the country, had never liked the system. He had always regarded it as a device to block his political advancement and keep power in the hands of the chiefs and, through them, of the government. He regarded the chiefs as government stooges, and their administrative system as one designed to perpetuate the colonial status of the country. This criticism was unfair, but it clearly indicated what would happen if men with this outlook achieved power under independence—as they did. Without delay they abolished the entire system.

A sound African economy was essential to the success of our political experiment. Political autonomy without economic independence is valueless and meaningless; and economic independence for an African country could only be achieved through the individual African cultivator. The economy of the Territory was entirely agricultural, except for a few scattered mines; therefore, the African had to become the primary producer of marketable crops if he were to enjoy the full fruits of his labour and create wealth for his community.

In our efforts to promote this policy we were hampered, as in the political field, by the conditions we inherited from the Germans. Germany had regarded her East African colony not only as a political adjunct of the Reich but as a source of raw materials for her factories. Germans were to be the producers of these raw materials and Africans were to supply the labour. The idea that Africans themselves should grow such basic commodities as coffee, tea and cotton was to the German mind quite heretical. In furtherance of this German policy a large number of leasehold estates had

been created. The coastal belt from Tanga to Mikindani was
heavily studded with sisal plantations. In the coastal hinterland
rubber plantations were numerous, and when the bottom dropped
out of the rubber marker, these were converted to sisal. As no
estate, sisal or rubber, of less than 2,000 acres was economically
viable, a very extensive area was absorbed by these European
holdings, and little land was left for African development. There
was a heavy demand on the African to supply the labour for these
enterprises. Every estate carried at least 1,000 workers on its
books—this number being necessary to cover sickness, desertion
and other causes of absenteeism. A minimum of 300 men per day
was required to keep an estate in production. Except for the processes of decorticating the sisal leaf, cleaning the fibre and com-
pressing it into bales, every operation was done by hand.

The extensive coffee and tea estates in the highlands of the
Territory also required labour in plenty for cultivating, weeding
and picking the crops. The local African was under constant
pressure to work on the estates near his village. He had little chance
to develop his own land, and often he could only do so if he bound
himself to work for the European owner whenever called upon.
This state of affairs smacked of the feudalism that Europe had
known in the fifteenth century.

There was little we could do about it. The Mandatory Power
was obliged to honour these leaseholds and offer them by auction
to potential purchasers as ex-enemy property. Many of them were
re-purchased by their former German owners who had succeeded
in returning to the Territory under a variety of non-German
passports. Others were purchased by people of Greek, Italian,
British, Australian and other nationalities. Having accepted cash
for these properties the Tanganyika Government felt itself morally
obliged to help the new owners with their labour problems—help
that could only be given at the expense of our policy of developing
an independent African economy. Serious possibilities of friction
existed between a Planters' Association determined to secure an
adequate supply of labour for its members and the officers of an
administration equally determined to honour the principle of the
Mandate and promote the cause of the African producer. In the
skirmishes between planters and District Commissioners the former
were not always the losers. The Tanganyika Planters' Association,
as we have seen, carried great weight and, in collaboration with
its Kenya counterpart, could exert strong pressure on East African
governments, locally and through financial interests in London.
More than once, plans to increase African production had to yield
to the labour requirements of certain big estate-holding companies.

Some of these estates represented large financial interests in London and elsewhere, which it required courage amounting to rashness to oppose.

It was obvious to everyone in the administration that if we were to continue the German policy of nursing the planters to the prejudice of the interests of the African producers, we would not only be infringing the mandatory principle but restricting the expansion of the Territory's revenue. The African was the main contributor of direct taxation through the Hut-and-Poll Tax. The Europeans had paid no direct tax of any kind before the war. If, therefore, a large proportion of the Poll Tax revenue were to come from wages earned on European estates, this revenue would remain stagnant or even be threatened if prices fell. This happened in the early 1930s. Wages on the sisal estates were slashed by 30 per cent, African labourers had serious difficulties in paying their taxes, and there would have been a calamitous drop in tax revenue if we had not devised the card system of payment by instalments. Even so, a number of planters did not operate the system honestly, and the Government was for a long time financially embarrassed. This position could never have arisen if our economy had been based on an all-African production. The estates were the weak link which brought us near to bankruptcy.

Under the reduced wage system an African was paid 12 shillings for thirty days' work or 144 shillings for a year's work. Since no African would ever work a full thirty-day month, his annual earnings never exceeded 100 shillings. On the other hand an African spending two months on his own cotton plot could bring back 100 shillings from a cotton market, as we proved in Korogwe and elsewhere. The rest of his time was his own to grow food for the sustenance of himself and his family. Moreover, by working for himself he could pay his tax in one lump sum, whereas it took him five or six months to pay if he relied on plantation wages. Neighbouring Uganda, where all production was in the hands of the indigenous African, suffered none of our setbacks during this time of crisis, and easily weathered the storm.

The lessons of the depression were not lost on us. Active steps were taken to promote African production. The estates had now to turn to recruiting workers from the interior or from outside territories. Our policy of turning the African into a primary producer, working for his own profit, went ahead. Cotton production on a large scale was promoted in the lowlands, where climate and soil were both favourable. In the higher altitudes, coffee growing had already been established, and each area had its own marketing organisation. Tea growing was still exclusively European, and any

attempt to create a body of African growers would have been
blocked by the then existing international restrictions on area
expansion, devised to prevent over-production and keep the price
steady. Other primary products handled by Africans were groundnuts, copra, hides and a small amount of tobacco.

The position of the African producer was gradually improving,
and his numbers were on the increase, until the war halted progress
with its drain on African manhood and the general disruption of
world trade. The Territory would have been better placed to
withstand the shock of war if it had enjoyed the same conditions as
Uganda. In my journal I made this record of a visit to Kampala
in 1943:

> Uganda generally has a polished, finished appearance, thanks
> mainly to its well-made, well-graded, well-drained roads, which
> are far superior to those of the other African colonies. The
> Africans, too, look far more prosperous than ours. This is especi-
> ally evident if you spend a morning in Kampala. The principal
> street of the town is an African Bond Street, with its crowds of
> gaily caparisoned, tall, well-nourished Uganda ladies doing their
> daily promenade among the shops, buying dress materials and
> other adornments. . . . These black, stately, full-breasted Junos
> garbed in silks that are girdled at the waist and flow around their
> ankles could not fail to attract the eye.

This was Uganda after many years of unimpeded British administration developed on the sound basis of a native economy. I was
comparing it with a Territory which had suffered years of exploitation and neglect before we took it over, and where much leeway
had to be made up.

The aftermath of German policy was not our only difficulty. The
resources at our disposal were meagre. With a large territory, much
of it uninhabitable, a thin and scattered population, poor communications open for only a part of the year and limited production,
the tax yield was unavoidably low. From this flowed a multitude
of ills—inadequate medical services, large areas infested with
tsetse-fly and closed to livestock, trade and transport restricted to a
limited season, widespread disease and low living standards. It was
a vicious circle and the only way to break it was a massive compaign
of agricultural production by Africans.

We eventually accepted this argument and applied it—but later
than we might have done. We had first to suffer the blizzard of the
price-drop in European-produced crops before we gave our real
attention to African production. We had ignored the lesson offered
to us by Uganda and Nigeria — that those colonies were the

wealthiest and most prosperous in which primary production was controlled by the indigenous population. We did not face up to the fact until it was nearly too late that European plantations, if allowed to dictate policy, could seriously endanger an African country's economy.

Apart from the African coffee developments in Bukoba and Moshi, the full campaign of African production did not get under way until 1933-4. It made fair headway until interrupted by the war: hundreds of miles of new roads were constructed; new areas were opened for trade; there was a considerable expansion of the Territory's budget, which allowed for more and better services and more money for the Native Treasuries; and there was a general air of improvement and prosperity.

The question has now to be asked: was our administration beneficial to the Africans of Tanganyika? Politically, was our revival of the hereditary principle, after nearly thirty years of a contrary German policy, a sensible course or an anachronism? We believed at the time that the concept of Indirect Rule was sound and honourable in its intention to restore an original culture which the Germans had sought to eradicate. It worked successfully in Nigeria and Uganda, and there was no reason to suppose that it would not also work in Tanganyika. We did not contemplate the possibility that a long spell of determined German policy might have so blunted the image of tribal government in African eyes as to rob it of reality, or that in reviving the principle we were trying to breathe life into very old bones. However right our conception, valid our motives or honourable our intentions, the fact remains that the new rulers of an independent Tanzania rejected the system and all that it represented.

On the economic front we were slow to appreciate the truth that people who are to be prepared for eventual political autonomy must be given a sound economic basis—or, put more simply, taught to create their own economic welfare. This applies with particular force to a country of which the economy is basically agricultural. A people cannot progress if they are only wage-earners. Under a plantation system wealth is concentrated in the hands of a few, and the majority are simply hewers of wood and drawers of water. It was such a system that we inherited from the Germans, and to replace it by something more equitable and beneficial to the country as a whole was easier to envisage in theory than to put into practice. However, until it was replaced or modified there could be no real material advancement of the indigenous peoples. If we were to treat the interests of Africans as paramount, as the Mandate laid down, we could not indefinitely maintain a 'lame duck' policy towards the plantation owners. That the Government or the administration had for a time to adopt this policy was forced upon us by circumstances over which we had little control. However, it was to everyone's credit that the policy was gradually changed, and that by the early 1930s we were promoting African production as fast as we could. It was a pity we did not begin earlier; nevertheless we laid the basis of continuing prosperity for the Africans of Tanganyika.

AUTOBIOGRAPHICAL EPILOGUE

This book is not an autobiography. Its purpose is to describe the methods of administration formerly employed by the British in dealing with African tribes, as seen at close range by a junior member of the Colonial Administrative Service. Nevertheless readers might like to know something about my background, and how I came to enter the Service.

My background was lower-middle-class. My father had a small bakery and grocery business in a country town south of Dublin. As the youngest of four sons I was destined for the family business. The brother next to me went to Canada at the age of fifteen. The two elder boys had a medical training, but there were no funds available to give me more than a rudimentary education.

At the age of four I went to a small local school staffed by three sisters. It had about thirty pupils ranging in age from four to fifteen. These women were first-class at the job: their school produced pupils who were to graduate in the various professions or serve with distinction in the civil or military services. We received a thorough grounding in the normal curriculum: maths, English, history, classics, modern languages and so on. The foundations of knowledge were well laid, and whatever academic success I achieved later I largely owe to the instruction I received from those three women.

Discipline was severe and order strictly maintained in school hours. Frivolity or inattention were punished corporally. There were three classes. Each class sat on either side of a long table, with the presiding teacher at one end. The teacher had a cane at her right hand reaching the entire length of the table. Every pupil was, therefore, within range of this punitive instrument. Stupid answers, lack of attention or any indication that the offender had not done his homework earned a crack on the knuckles or the shoulders.

After eight or nine years of tuition from the three sisters my father decided to send me to a Dublin boarding school so that I could undergo a toughening process before entering his business. There was no entrance examination to be passed before admission to an Irish school. If your parents were respectable and could pay the fees, you were admitted. On my first morning at the new school I was wandering around the main hall, feeling very much the raw boy up

174

from the country and waiting to be assigned to a class, when I noticed a number of boys going into a room and seating themselves at desks. I asked a master what was going on in that room and he replied that the boys were sitting for the annual scholarship examination. I asked if I could enter. "Of course", he said. I went into the room and sat with the others. The examination lasted two days. Thanks to the three sisters, I won by a comfortable margin the first of the two scholarships awarded, which came from an endowment by a former pupil and were good for four years. The winning of this scholarship changed my father's attitude to my future and he told me that I could aim for a university career if my progress at this school showed signs that I could make the grade.

I improved my credit with my father by winning exhibitions in the junior and middle grades and the modern history medal in the latter. My entry into Dublin University was jeopardised by a serious illness during my last year at school. I was too ill to sit for an entrance exhibition for which I had put in several months' work. However, after a long convalescence at home I recovered sufficiently to enter in the Michaelmas term of 1919, admittance being granted on the strength of my examination record at school. By this time my Canadian brother, who had come to Europe with a Canadian infantry battalion and survived the war, was persuaded to stay at home and enter the family business, so all was well from that point of view. My two eldest brothers were army doctors with established careers, and I was about to enter Trinity College, Dublin, not knowing what the future had in store for me when I had completed my four years in that institution. My programme was to read for an honours degree in classics and law.

Throughout my life I have been fortunate in finding help when it was most needed. I have already acknowledged my debt to the three sisters for the education they gave me in my early boyhood. I had now come to man's estate and was about to grapple with the testing experience of a college career. The guidance I would now require was of a more sophisticated kind. It came in the person of my classical master in Dublin. At school he had encouraged my studies in Latin and Greek, and boosted my morale by persuading me that I was not lacking in intelligence. He continued to assist me after I entered the University with special coaching sessions to supplement my tutorials; and thanks to his unselfish and invaluable counsel, I succeeded in my second year in winning the Trinity Scholarship, the highest academic award to which an undergraduate could aspire.

The financial and other benefits of the scholarship were considerable. It covered almost the whole of an undergraduate's fees and commitments, and included free commons and free beer. The scholar could augment his scholarship by reciting the Latin grace at Commons for a fee of £10 a year, a lot of money at that time. The scholar also became a parliamentary elector. The accolade of the parliamentary franchise reflected the Board's attitude towards a Scholar of the House: he was regarded as a person of mature intelligence who could be trusted to make a valid judgment on matters of public importance. He even wore a silk gown of graduate pattern to distinguish him from the rest. He enjoyed a further privilege that marked him as a person of superior character and sense of responsibility: whereas the ordinary resident under-graduate was obliged to answer roll call nightly at 9 p.m., the scholar could stay out of college until midnight. However, at the time of which I write, this privilege was rarely enjoyed. Fighting between the King's forces and the I.R.A. was going on around us day by day, and the civilian population was often at risk. When darkness fell the wise man kept indoors. One winter's evening at about 8 o'clock I was walking down Grafton Street with a fellow-student on my way back to college and happened to laugh at some remark he made. The next moment I felt a gun pressed into my stomach and a voice said "I'll teach you to laugh." We had been accosted by two "Black and Tans" (auxiliary police). I received several prods from a loaded revolver, which I thought would go off at any moment. Both of us were thoroughly frisked, but eventually persuaded these men that we were not I.R.A. gunmen and were allowed to go our way. It was a long time before I again ventured into the Dublin streets at night.

In September of 1922 I graduated with a Senior Moderatorship in classics and in the following year took a degree in law. My problem now was to find a job. My preference was for the Bar, but this necessitated private means to see one through the early years of struggle, and these I did not possess. The Civil Service seemed the only alternative.

We had a very efficient Appointments Committee in Trinity; its recommendations, as well as the standing of our Dublin degrees, carried weight. Thanks to its efforts I was offered a First Grade appointment in the North of Ireland division of the Home Civil Service, and this I decided to accept. My name had also gone forward to the Colonial Office and I had been interviewed by one of its representatives. I did not, however, place much confidence in this application and banished it from my mind when the H.C.S. accepted me. My appointment was due to begin in September of 1923 and I lived in my college rooms until the day I was to leave for Belfast.

After 1921 it was not considered safe for a Trinity student to visit his country home. We were all regarded by the I.R.A. as adherents of the "British enemy" and more than one of our alumni had been murdered on vacation in the country. The position was no better after the formation of the Irish Free State in 1922 because the I.R.A. then turned its wrath against the new Irish Government, and all who rendered it obedience were suspect; so I, for one, preferred the comparative safety of my rooms in Trinity.

On the morning of my departure I saw the College postman in the distance and went across to say good-bye. He asked me if I had received my letter that morning. I replied that there had been no letter. He assured me that there was one. To resolve the matter we both went to my rooms and there I showed him the empty letter box.

"I must have put it in the corresponding door upstairs," he said; and so he had. It was a bulky envelope with an O.H.M.S. postmark and inside was a letter offering me the appointment of a cadet administrator, in the Mandated Territory of Tanganyika. After several hours of pondering the problem, I decided to accept the job, being moved to this decision by a variety of considerations: the lure of distant lands; the prospect of working among African races—an unknown and possibly exciting experience; but what finally tilted the balance towards Africa was the prospect of getting away from the political environment of fanaticism and strife in which I had spent my college years. In Africa, at least, there would be peace.

The same day I contacted the Colonial Office doctor in Dublin and had my medical examination. Only when he had passed me fit for tropical service did I send a letter of resignation to Belfast and a letter of acceptance to London. Evidently the Mandated Territory of Tanganyika was impatient for my services because I sailed for Africa three weeks later having joined the Colonial Service through my accidental meeting with a college postman.

Including routine home leaves before the 1939 war I had served in Africa for approximately twenty-two years when I returned home for the last time in the late summer of 1945. People have asked what were my impressions of post-war England after my years abroad. When I first had left home, conditions in England were good. The country was recovering from the First World War; supplies were plentiful and cheap; there was a general air of goodwill and prosperity; and money had real value. To give a concrete instance— the 25 shillings a week that my father allowed me sufficed for my breakfast and lunch daily, my cricket and other club subscriptions, my college servant's wages and an occasional visit to the theatre. True, I speak of conditions in Dublin, but they also applied across the water. Relations between the British and Irish Governments had become more friendly and travel between the two countries was unrestricted.

The English scene was different when I came home in 1945. I was struck by the pallid countenances and ill-nourished condition of people and their abruptness of manner. There was an air of listlessness about them—not to be wondered at if one thought of the sleepless nights and the ever-present possibility of violent death from bombs and rockets that had confronted them in the seemingly endless war. The children looked fitter than their parents, perhaps because they were given the lion's share of the available food; more likely because the child has the capacity to forget. But, above all, the destruction in and around London brought home to me the intensity with which the German Air Force had bombed the city and its citizens. If any colonial officer had thought he was being ill used by fate in having to serve in a tropical climate for many years without respite, he now had to see his experiences in perspective comparing them to what the people of England had been enduring so long.

Although I had been born and bred in Ireland I decided to make my home in England, where my loyalties were centred. I was a British citizen by birth and held a British passport. There were, of course, difficulties for my kind of immigrant. With exiguous resources and a totally inadequate pension I had the problem of housing and maintaining a family. Houses were five times their pre-war price and hard to come by; and jobs were scarce unless you had a suitable qualification. There was no market in England for men whose training had been confined to colonial administration. So I had, as it were, to go back to school. I took a two-year course in advertising and salesmanship with a London technical college and at the same time was glad to get a subordinate job in an advertising agency at £6 a week. Through a friendly solicitor whom I met by chance I managed to purchase a house on the instalment plan. However, opportunity knocks for most of us at least once, and it knocked for me—whereupon my circumstances in the commercial world improved greatly, and the grim spectre of poverty faded. From then until my retirement a few years ago, I enjoyed a productive if strenuous existence.